MAD ABOUT THE BOY

MAD ABOUT THE BOY

The Life and Times of Boy George and Culture Club

Anton Gill

CENTURY PUBLISHING

LONDON

Copyright © Anton Gill 1984

All rights reserved
First published in Great Britain in 1984
by Century Publishing Co. Ltd
Portland House
12-13 Greek Street London W1V 5LE

ISBN 0 7126 0983 0

Designed and produced by
Michael Balfour Ltd
3 Wedgwood Mews
Greek Street
London W1V 5LW

Project co-ordinator	Michael Balfour
Picture editor	Nicki Blackett-Ord
Picture research	Sue Leighton
Designers	Field Wylie & Company
Typesetting	H & J Graphics Ltd
Reproduction	Gilchrist Brothers Ltd
Printing and binding	Ebenezer Baylis & Son Ltd

CONTENTS

	Prologue	8
1	'DO YOU REALLY WANT TO HURT ME?' 'I rode to fame on my voice.'	12
2	RECENT HIGHS 'They found me very traditional in Japan. Very cultural.'	20
3	BLACK AND WHITE POP FOR CHILD EARS 'Culture Club is important to me. It's like a family.'	30
4	THE BOYS IN THE BAND 'The thing about a band, four people, is that you have to kind of delegate ideas and you also have to make things available for other people.'	40
5	SCHOOL, SEX AND STYLE 'It's difficult for people to understand me. Although I look obvious, there's much more to me than people see.'	50
6	MAD ABOUT THE BOY 'My personality is what sold me.'	62
7	IMITATORS 'I am a show-off, and that's that. That's how I see myself, and that's how I like to be seen. But it's not all down to the clothes I wear.'	72
8	THE LOOK 'Everyone says that I will grow out of this some day, that I will look back in ten years from now and think how stupid I looked. The truth is the opposite.'	78
9	TALK ABOUT THE BOY 'People think I'm going to be some sort of idiot pouf who's going to be completely gormless.'	90
10	CULTURE CLUB 'It's multicultural. I'm Jewish, George is Catholic and dresses up, Mikey is black and Roy is like a typical English boy.' (Jon)	100
11	THE FANS 'I'm sure the girls weren't intending to tear us limb from limb – at least, I hope not!'	110
12	PASS IT ON AFRICA 'I'm trying to open people's minds and make them more tolerant of things which aren't harmful.'	118
	The BG and CC Quiz	124
	Culture Clubography	126

PROLOGUE

On 10th June 1984 Madame Tussaud's, the famous London waxworks museum, unveiled a new effigy in its Hall of Heroes. The figure sits casually dressed in a motley tartan outfit with platform shoes, hands clasped round the left ankle. The make-up has been meticulously applied; the pushed-up black hat, worn high on the back of the head, sits perfectly on immaculate plaits, which are tied back with a printed white band and fall in plaits to the shoulders.

Thus it was that four days before his twenty-third birthday, Boy George, singer and songwriter with Culture Club, received public confirmation that he had become a British national institution. You know that you've really 'arrived', when your likeness stands shoulder to shoulder with the nation's famous as a main attraction at Madame Tussaud's.

With the possible exception of Michael Jackson, George Alan O'Dowd is the biggest star in Eighties pop music. With his outrageous dress sense and androgynous ways, it didn't take long before this self-confessed 'gender bender' was hogging the media headlines from New York to Tokyo, whichever way round the world you travelled.

The way he looked at first caused confusion. Everyone thought he was a girl. His response was the masterstroke: he merely added Boy to his name – and stayed ambiguous. Soon came the questions concerning *his* sexual inclinations – is he or isn't he?/does he or doesn't he?; a worldwide investigation was under way. With the rumours still flying, and of course The Boy does nothing to discourage them, it has been George's love of the camera, and the camera's seeming response to his ever-changing flamboyance, that has consistently kept him on the front pages. Well, that and the stream of brilliant Culture Club records.

Video arrived at exactly the right time for Boy George. His appearance, coupled with his pure, sweet voice, make him ideal for the music video age, with its relentless emphasis on image and style, and after all (which is a main point) George has spent enough time in front of mirrors to know precisely how to use his. With video you can be in lots of different places at the same time, and so somewhere in the world, be it day or night, a video machine is playing George's song. He and Culture Club are everywhere.

The furthest he goes is to skip across the stage, smiling fondly. In short, The Boy is simply not sexy, or at least not in any obvious way. Talk to him about the subject and he says, 'Sex? No thank you. I'd rather have a nice cup of tea.' And it's easy to believe that he really would.

The Boy, as a person, may be a living work of art, but there is something about him which is 'easy' for lots of people to identify with. Unlike chart rivals Duran Duran, for example, who have a mainly teenage following,

Culture Club appeal right across generations. Underneath the glittering façade, there is something ordinary, sincere and even level-headed about Boy George, almost as if he were an eccentric member of a universal family. Appearances apart, he has a reputation for being puritanical, and he is certainly sensible about drugs which he wouldn't touch 'with a barge pole'. He has also denounced casual sex, the one-night stands, and the unhappiness they can bring.

His popularity has, in many places, had the effect of sending machismo into the closet, to the extent that many teenage boys now wear prettier clothes than their girlfriends. It's a lot easier to look like The Boy than Burt Reynolds or Clint Eastwood. One London headmistress isn't too impressed however. 'People like Boy George warp the minds of adolescent boys growing up.' But it's not just the boys. Alongside the Boy George clones are the Girl George clones (though it can be hard to tell them apart), and in newspapers there have even been reported cases of Granny George clones. Somehow George manages to appeal to both sexes, and everyone in between. Has a star ever had so many lookalikes? (And cloning must be the sincerest form of flattery.)

A couple of years ago Boy George was a penniless social butterfly flitting around the London scene, and most often to be found at the famous Blitz Club (where the only way you could guarantee entrance at the door was by looking like Greto Garbo or coming as the mad King Ludwig of Bavaria). George always got in at a time when he particularly favoured dressing up as a nun and describing himself as 'the immaculate conception'.

George has moved on since those days. Having teamed up with a bunch of musicians, he formed Culture Club, a band whose name reflects a willingness to 'borrow' music and image from every source. After passing an audition, during which George told a prominent record company executive to stop nodding his head and listen to the music instead, and then signing to the Virgin Records label, Culture Club have risen and risen, with reported controversy never far from the headlines and failure unencountered. Currently Boy George is working on a book called *The Day I Married The World*, which documents his response to international media and its response to him and the Club.

But, if the Boy George extravaganza is to run and run, and he is to keep his place in the Hall of Heroes, it depends on the intelligence and musical ability of Culture Club collectively. A brilliant image is the perfect vehicle to grab initial attention, but success in the pop world has to be sustained through music.

Aware of how fast kings and queens are made and then broken on the wheel of the pop world, Madame Tussaud's give their new model a life

PROLOGUE

expectancy of three to five years. George is a realist. He accepts that one day he may have to be melted down – but, if this ever happens, he says, with that disarming smile, he hopes he will be transformed into a model of Oscar Wilde. He also points out that he is a singer and not just a 'freak', so there is every chance that he will be around for years to come.

Staring at his wax *alter ego* on that day in June 1984 he declared, 'It looks like me, I'm very pleased'. His only worry seemed to be that his constantly evolving style (the famous black hat was abandoned the previous February, the plaits forsaken soon after and then came the blond hair) would make the effigy seem dated. No matter. The waxwork embodies the look that took Boy George to the top of the charts and the media interest tree in little less than eighteen months. The image is a crystallisation of a moment in world pop history; *Mad About The Boy* is a celebration of that moment and what it means.

'I like everyone. I'm sure I'm in love with the whole world, but I just get brassed off with people because they let themselves down so much.'

1

'DO YOU REALLY WANT TO HURT ME?'

'I rode to fame on my voice.'

1982 didn't start too well for Culture Club. On May 21st Virgin Records, the company with which they had signed, released their first single, WHITE BOY. Although it failed to chart, the solid musicianship of the band was evident and the song itself was well constructed with a moody trio and all the warmth one associates with Culture Club. The song fell down, though, on its repetitiousness and the fact that George was still unprepared to really let go on his singing. The lyrics carried the first seeds of the Culture Club philosophy since the 'white' of the title has more to do with being a conformist than the colour of his skin.

WHITE BOY was paid little attention by the music press, despite (because of?!) the fact that George was already a familiar figure round the club and fashion circuit. Perhaps jealous of his reputation, music hacks tended to dismiss him and the band as mannequins for exotic clothes rather than the serious musicians, who might have helped the writers in their quest to establish personal fame. A recurring adjective used by critics for the band at this time was 'shallow'.

Nothing daunted, the band released a second single just over a month later, on June 25th. This was in keeping with the Virgin policy of firing out singles regularly until a hit was registered; Virgin had great faith in their new signings. I'M AFRAID OF ME followed its predecessor into the remainder baskets, but it was a more assured song, taking a steel band sound as its basis though still in a funky vein. And the main thing was that George's voice was sounding good.

Both these singles were quite different from most of the music around at the time, when many other bands were following a fashion which decreed that the more exclusive a band was, the better it had to be. Cultivating an aloof or elitist attitude could really help a band, as could a cool stance and words which rang with a certain disdain, then called 'style'. WHITE BOY and I'M AFRAID OF ME weren't afraid to be emotionally warm, and the fact that they failed to score can probably be attributed to public doubt; people weren't sure whether they ought to like a band like Culture Club.

Question marks were beginning to hover over the new band, as always happens when instant success fails to materialise in such a 'here today and gone tomorrow' industry as the music business. Things seemed balanced against them. Even their colourful image seemed to have introduced a prejudice against the music; their great head start seemed to be hindering rather than helping. George grew despondent. Pop music needs a constant updating of images but Culture Club seemed to have made an excessive leap. Nobody had seen anything quite like them before, especially anything quite like Boy George ... though the public was by now quite used to the make-up of

David Bowie or the showmanship of Elton John. The music was fine, but who was it aimed at?

There seemed to be a disparity between their extreme appearance and the melodic tunes they produced. Where was the alienating sound to match the look? Weren't they friends of Steve Strange and the weird Blitz crowd? Some said the music was falling between two stools – rock and middle-of-the-road. But if the music was middle-of-the-road, how could it be sold to the MOR audience once they knew what Boy George looked like?

About three months went by before the next release. On September 3rd 1982 their new single came out and it was a case of third time lucky for George, Jon, Roy and Mikey. Like Lord Byron before them, the band awoke one morning to find themselves famous.

DO YOU REALLY WANT TO HURT ME?, a sweet-sounding lovers' rock tune, with plaintive lyrics that directly related to the misfit singer, drifted into the lower reaches of the UK chart, then zoomed to the Number One position on October 19th, where it remained for all of fifteen weeks. In the year of ET, Steven Spielberg's hugely successful film, there was still room for yet another 'cuddly creature from another planet' in the public heart.

The song was the breakthrough Culture Club needed and really it had to be: it was a classic song which nothing could have stopped from becoming successful. It was also a blow to a British music scene which was becoming increasingly insular and arrogant, since the words entreated affection, the music was easygoing and melodic and, above all, the singing was as beautiful as the idea behind the song was daring. Culture Club and their songs were accessible; people soon realised this and flocked to buy the single.

What Boy George has called 'plagiarism' is there, but the influences, musical and lyrical, that shape the song have been assimilated for his own purposes, in order to create a sound of his own, more exactly Culture Club's own. 'Nobody creates things, everything you see is a complete rip-off of something else. If you're not influenced by everything, you must be a complete moron', is a sentiment which George is fond of echoing.

DO YOU REALLY WANT TO HURT ME? is still one of their greatest songs, and musically their most complex. At one time, Boy George suggested – tongue-in-cheek as usual – it was probably the only proper song Culture Club had, with proper chord sequences and keyboard changes in it. 'It's just very musical. I think it's a very well-constructed song', added the Boy with disarming candour.

The success of DO YOU REALLY WANT TO HURT ME? was not confined to the UK market and it soon took on the world, territory by territory. DO YOU REALLY WANT TO HURT ME? was released in 52 countries and stormed to Number One in 51 of these. Only in the US, the biggest record market in the world, did it fail to top the charts and there it reached Number Two, which is good going for a band with a singer like Boy George in a country of Marlboro men where people really believe in the apparent virtues of John Wayne. Some say that Americans had reservations about the precise meaning of the words in the song ('my gentle little song' – George), others say that certain US citizens, not to mention citizens from elsewhere, did want to hurt him and, as we shall see, his receptions abroad have varied from warm to overheated. The point, though, is that love conquers all and George loves everyone, and so he was bound to conquer America, and so he did. More on this later.

Success thrust the group into the public eye. DO YOU REALLY WANT TO HURT ME? became BBC Radio 2's 'Record Of The Week', an honour usually reserved for the likes of Neil Diamond, Buck's Fizz or Barry Manilow. Thus Culture Club were in with the 'out' club, but the odd thing is that they also became hip for London's *beau monde*. It should be remembered that BBC Radio 2's listeners liked the sound of Culture Club rather than the band's image, and it wasn't until the band appeared on Top Of The Pops, the UK's major TV chart show, that the general public saw Boy George in full glory for the first time. The reaction was amazement.

'Most people who dress up are really nervous. I'm not. I suppose I'm an old-timer.'

The press had a field day all the next week, but as we, and especially Boy George, all know, 'if there is one thing worse than being talked about, it is not being talked about' and the single immediately flourished amid the small storm whipped up by the press. One Sunday paper called George the 'Wally of the week', but conceded that he was beautifully made up. Media talk, even before the appearance on Top Of The Pops, had centred round the question of whether George was a boy or a girl and, if no answer could be found, would 'Miss or Mr Weirdo' do as the correct mode of address? Column inches were filled with the debate. 'Disgusted of Luton' seethed his way into the letter columns on the subject, while fans leapt to George's defence with short fiery notes that said 'leave him alone'. What the whole fracas revealed was that some people were getting very worked up about the way someone chose to dress. Some people were very uptight!

The next single, TIME (CLOCK OF THE HEART) was released on November 19th 1982 and reached the Number Three position in the UK

chart by December 14th. The fury was abating and the harsh comments were dying off, though a few remained. The truth was that the press was getting used to Boy George and its scribblers were now reduced to using the word 'outrageous' about him, an adjective that has settled on his career like a blessing. It's no bad thing to be 'outrageous', though try telling 'Disgusted of Luton' that.

Even at the start, when he could have lost his nerve, Boy George proved astute in handling the press. And he learnt fast, too, how best to milk the headlines. He capitalised on the fuss over his sexual identity without ever making a fool of himself, instinctively teasing out the publicity for as long as he could. To this day he has never settled the question and it is the questioners themselves who have often looked fools.

This policy of preserving his ambiguous position has worked out for him brilliantly well, and it has worked out because he has never gone for the cheap shot in gaining attention but always preferred to stick to the long-term strategy, which he has consistently advised everyone else to follow. 'I couldn't care less if people think I am a girl', he said at the time of hottest debate. Boy George's strategy is to be himself at all times and he feels that everyone else should be true to their own selves too.

In effect, the Boy George philosophy says, 'Here I am, this is what I look like, these are the things I like and even if I'm inconsistent, you can't categorise me. Keep people guessing, keep them intrigued. Be honest and ignore what anyone else thinks of you.' All this apparent sincerity and public honesty has paid off as brilliant publicity for George, but it has earned him wry looks, too.

As one paper put it, 'Rebel George Is Laughing All The Way To The Bank', a dry but not necessarily unsympathetic view one might take. Whether George is a rebel is quite another. If he is, then he is a subtler one than the rebels who have gone before him in the pop world, since his (convenient?) credo is that a revolution can only truly be accomplished by changing society from within, not by knocking the whole structure down from the outside and then rebuilding with the rubble. It's a sane approach and one society seems ready to accept; it's certainly one that is popular.

But it is songs that open the doors Culture Club constantly walk through. Without the songs, there would be no keys. Where other bands have pretensions, Culture Club rely on the beliefs which they convey in their songs and it is these beliefs which have crossed generations and made them so popular. They have achieved something which only one group, The Beatles, has done before them and that is to appeal to people of all ages. And that is despite George's looks. But then, George has the power to disarm the most

'DO YOU REALLY WANT TO HURT ME?'

disapproving of people. His looks gain attention; his manner charms.

DO YOU REALLY WANT TO HURT ME? has sold more than 6½ million copies and justified Virgin Records' faith in Culture Club. DO YOU REALLY WANT TO HURT ME? provided a base of popularity for the album, KISSING TO BE CLEVER, which was launched as early as October 3rd 1982. Signing Culture Club has clearly paid off in a big way. The album went Platinum in the UK, and Gold in Australia, Japan, Germany, France, New Zealand, Canada and the USA and has clocked up total sales of more than 3 million. This followed DO YOU REALLY WANT TO HURT ME? (the single), which went Platinum in the UK and France and Gold in Australia, Belgium, Denmark, Holland, New Zealand, Switzerland, Canada and the USA.

At the end of 1982, George summed things up like this: 'If we were the fashionable trendies we are accused of being, then our first two singles would have skanked to Number One without any trouble.'

He was being over-defensive. Everyone knew by now the band was great and the second half of 1982 had more than made up for the first half. Things were moving so fast that Culture Club hardly knew where they were going any more. But one thing was sure: Culture Club had arrived with a capital A.

II

RECENT HIGHS

'They found me very traditional in Japan. Very cultural.'

'Boy! Boy! Boy! Boy!' yell the ecstatic Japanese fans after a concert at Japan's second city, Osaka, as George, dressed in white and wearing a wedding veil, pads away backstage to the waiting van, which will sweep him away from the screaming mob. East meets West, and this time it is the West that is proving the more inscrutable, as George drives off, face still concealed under the wedding veil.

A week after the ceremony at Madame Tussaud's, Culture Club were revisiting Japan on the first leg of a two-month tour, also to embrace Australia. The band were playing two dates at the enormous Osaka Castle Sports Hall before moving on to Nagoya to play the packed National Exhibition Hall. These dates were only a preparation for their important concerts at Tokyo's Budokan, a venue which has been played by all the major rock stars, from Bob Dylan to the Rolling Stones, and which was sold out for each of the Club's three performances.

George loved Japan. He spent hours wandering around the ornamental gardens, shopping for kimonos and eating sushi at Japanese restaurants. He also seemed to enjoy his visit to a Japanese tea ceremony, but then you can imagine that it's the sort of thing that would be right up his street.

Japan returned Boy George's compliment and fell in love with him. Everywhere you looked in the streets of the cities there were posters of him, most television programmes seemed to be interrupted by the Culture Club advertisement for Nissan cars (where they sing Miss Me Blind) and many of the nation's youth, especially the girls, were dressed up just like George dolls.

Culture Club had been 'big in Japan' for some time but this visit made them positively huge. They seemed to have the country under some sort of a spell, where the presence of any member of the group in a street was enough to induce riots, whose first symptom was autograph fever followed by fainting fits, hysteria and fighting to get at The Club. Love for Culture Club in Japan has grown beyond that normally devoted to 'all things Western' over there.

There are many reasons for this. Japan is a country which loves ritual and costume and its Kabuki theatre has a tradition of men dressing up and wearing splendid make-up. What may be flamboyant 'cross-dressing' to the European observer may seem a reflection of Japan's cultural glories to the citizens of Tokyo and Kyoto ... even as modelled by George. Or perhaps it has something to do with George's artificial appearance, which is quite in tune with this highly stylised and mannered society.

Another argument runs thus: George represents individuality in a society which finds individuality unpardonable. Through George, Japanese fans can be vicariously individual, or at least support the notion of individuality and thus for a while be free of the oppressiveness of their society.

'It's funny,' says George, Geisha-like behind thick white face paint. 'I'm taking their ideas and giving them back to them. It's very confusing but I'm also very flattered.'

After the Budokan, Culture Club flew on to play in Brisbane, Melbourne and five days (all sold out) in Sydney, all the biggest concert halls in Australia, before returning to England in mid-July 1984. George says he never gets nervous before a concert – in fact the bigger, the better, and the Australian concerts were big enough to be very enjoyable for everyone concerned.

1984 had already been a busy year for the band. Between March 28th and April 23rd they had been back to the USA, and also Canada, where they were greeted by the kind of enthusiasm which The Beatles had experienced there some twenty years earlier. The plan was to play Montreal and Ottawa, then cross the border into the States for a tour which would be entirely different from their earlier two. This time they were going to avoid the bigger cities and play the medium-sized places they had previously left out. If everything worked out then Culture Club would have covered an enormous area of the country and thus secured their popularity throughout the land.

There were doubts, however, about playing many of the places on the USA itinerary; no one could be sure what the reaction would be to a group like Culture Club in the very conservative, and highly religious Mid West. How would the Bible belt, with its population of 'born-agains', take to the other members of a flamboyant English pop group, let alone the androgynous front person?

The tour of the USA was scheduled to begin in Buffalo (famous in nearby New York as being a place no one in their right mind would visit), go on through Pittsburgh and Detroit, 'The Motor City' and home of Tamla Motown, take in Cleveland and St Louis, stop by in Nashville, 'Home of Country Music', and then amble on to Miami Beach by way of Charlotte and Lakeland, two of the less well-known spots on the continent of North America. The outlook seemed distinctly unpromising despite Culture Club's conquest of the USA on their previous tours and their prominence in the charts. The questions seemed to be, would George's talent and charm be enough to take on American conservatism and win? Or could George keep cool under the collar in redneck country?

'Some Americans haven't accepted us at all. They are very worried about me', said George. And this was hardly an understatement: there were reports in American papers about spectators at Culture Club's concerts vomiting over the hideous appearance of Boy George, and others warning teachers of how Boy George was out to corrupt America's young.

The start of the tour could hardly be described as quiet. When the band arrived at London's Heathrow Airport, they found they had to run the gauntlet of thousands of fans, screaming and fighting for a glimpse of their departing heroes; screaming and fighting also for a lock of precious hair or a piece of Culture clothing. The fans were mainly girls and they were also mainly after George, who had to be protected from their advances.

Although many of the kids were dressed just as they thought their hero would be, there was no question of George getting lost in the crowd of clones because, as usual, he had kept several steps ahead of them. This time he was hatless and wore a multicoloured coat over a double-breasted tweed drape jacket in check, with splendid golfing socks, brilliant white sneakers on his size 10 feet and, as a final touch of elegance, a kilt which swung jauntily on his hips all the way up the steps to the plane ... and away from the clutches of his ever-persistent admirers. All in all, it wasn't a bad send-off – but it paled by comparison with what he was to find on the other side of the Atlantic.

First of all, Canada fell at George's feet and worshipped. Well, some of its pop fans did anyway: 3,000 screaming fans were at Montreal Airport to greet the band. The tour opened to two dates in Montreal over the weekend of March 31/April 1. Over 30,000 people came to see them, and a large proportion were dressed as George and sang along to all the songs. When IT'S A MIRACLE began, George was showered with roses and applauded to the skies. Even the stadium's staff were standing on seats at the back to catch the show.

Culture Club are popular all over the world but in Canada their popularity has reached saturation point. 200,000 fans applied for tickets for their tour but were disappointed at being unable to get any in what was a mad, mad rush. Culture Club are the first band ever to sell a million copies of an album in Canada. That album was COLOUR BY NUMBERS and it sold over three times the 300,000 copies required to make an album go Platinum in that country.

When they crossed the border into the USA, the reception was no less enthusiastic. In most places they visited the story was the same, but there were two incidents which marred an otherwise perfect tour and each of these involved Boy George clones.

The first involved a student of the Mormon Brigham Young University in Provo, Utah, called Ray Carter, who, inspired by the visit of Culture Club to his country, put on a burlesque act as 'Gay George': in itself a presumptuous comment on the Boy's sexuality. University elders decided that Boy George was in the USA to advocate homosexuality and transvestism, and all posters and records of the group were banned. This overreaction was reported in many American newspapers but the band were able to ignore it;

after all they were touring on the other side of the country. George told reporters there was something strange about a religious group which allows a man to have four wives yet clamps down on Culture Club's records.

The second clone turned up in Puerto Rico, at a time when the band were playing Atlanta, Georgia. This one signed autographs, gave interviews to San Juan newspapers and even appeared on a local television show before disappearing into the night.

Meanwhile George himself was busy encountering the famous – maybe that should be the equally famous – Michael Jackson, who phoned him and suggested doing a song together (an offer which George declined, feeling that then was not the time to do anything separately from Culture Club).

Next, in Pittsburgh, he found himself staying at the same hotel as Democratic contender for the presidency Senator Gary Hart: he of 'Where's The Beef' fame. This chance meeting seemed for a moment to be too good to pass up without a couple of publicity shots. Aides from both camps discussed the possibility of the two celebrities being photographed together. George proved willing although his own political leanings are strongest towards the Ecology Party.

Frantic meetings were held, aides mumbled together but finally word came down to the seventh floor, where Culture Club were staying, that Hart had to decline; obviously because he was unsure if being pictured next to George would win or lose him votes from the great American electorate. As it happened he soon lost the Democratic nomination to Walter Mondale and so was never given the chance to take over from Ronald Reagan at The White House.

That same evening, Culture Club took the stage at the Pittsburgh Civic Arena, where 13,000 yelled their delight at the band, even in a tough old steel town like Pittsburgh ... maybe Hart was overcautious in assessing the reaction of the American people.

All the publicity and the adulation did of course cause headaches for the band and the organisers of the tour. A major problem was the ticket touts who always seemed to be able to get tickets, however strictly their issue was controlled. At one venue, Cleveland, a couple of Flash Harrys went round offering $15 tickets for $500 and were only saved from

being lynched by some passing policemen.

Security was another difficult area. America is the home of the rock star assassin, a breed seldom found elsewhere. This, coupled with the enthusiasm of the fans, forced George to keep a low profile and the band to maintain a tight watch over security. Various hotel reservations were made in each town, and only at the last moment was one settled on. Then a whole floor was taken, and sealed off by security men. Fame can have its drawbacks.

Charlotte, North Carolina, is a conservative town in a conservative tobacco-growing state, but that didn't stop tickets for the band's concert there, at the 11,000-seat Coliseum, from selling out within a day of the box office opening. The city let its hair down for George's visit, perhaps reassured by George's statement, 'I know a lot of people think we are corrupting young people, but we're not ... I'm trying to open people's minds, and make them more tolerant of things that aren't harmful.'

'The statements I'm making are general statements and not arrogant. I'm not saying how to vote. I'm taking about things that affect ordinary people. I'm taking about feelings and emotions. About being individual and living up to your potential.'

George's message got across and Charlotte gave them a fingerlickin' good welcome. Roy said of the reception they got in North Carolina, 'We'd heard that Charlotte had a real redneck reputation, but we found no opposition. It just goes to show how popular our music is.'

It also shows how successful Culture Club have been at breaking down barriers – they just seem to melt away at their approach – and this means that the band is succeeding in another of its main aims: that there should be no barriers between people.

The fact that Culture Club have succeeded even in a ruggedly conservative country such as America, whose macho self-image is built on the idea of cowboys and frontiersmen, and where many people still don't realise John Wayne was only acting, is an indication not only of their exceptional talent but also of their ability to tailor their image to the expectations of people wherever they go. This without being untrue to themselves or compromising in any way. The ability to get on with everyone is a rare gift and it is one of which George in particular, the Karma Chameleon himself, has an instinctive grasp. Under that fey exterior, there is a shrewd man.

One last note about Charlotte. On the eve of the concert there, a Georgealike competition was held at the town's 2001 club and people were turned away in their hundreds. So much for George not being accepted.

At the end of the tour – a 26-day grind – Mikey, Roy and Jon came home exhausted and were met at Heathrow Airport by zealous customs officers. Mikey was detained for six hours and was obliged to pay £60 on a guitar he had bought in the States. Jon was delayed two hours and relieved of £30 duty on some new trousers. But Culture Club are not The Sex Pistols and refused to be fazed by the incident. 'It was purely routine. The Customs men were very good', said Mikey diplomatically. Jon shrugged it off with 'Customs always do this with bands'. George himself hasn't always been that cool about the officers of HM Customs and Excise, and perhaps it was lucky that he'd stayed behind on this occasion to watch Liberace in his New York show. He has been misquoted in the *Daily Star* as having called customs officers 'pigs', when he had actually referred to them as 'obnoxious'. Back in November 1983 he had another run in with them and – so the story goes – blew his top at a security guard at Heathrow after he kept setting off the metal detector. After three journeys through it, nothing could be found. 'It must be my ring of confidence', joked George when he finally saw the funny side of the situation.

Although Boy George says he'd never leave England to become a tax exile, or for any other reason, because he loves it so much, the rest of the world is claiming a lot of his time these days. From Tokyo to Sydney, from New York to Athens, thousand of fans – of both sexes – are dressing up imitating his appearance and aiming to adopt something of his approach to life. In many ways his gentle beliefs can be compared to those of the Flower Children in the late Sixties, and even his clothes remind one of those flowing garments of that period. This may be a false comparison: it has of course been suggested that the choice of flowing robes is a ploy to conceal his less than ideally shaped body and also that he is hardly likely to ever make a declaration eschewing the material things of the world, not with his surely overflowing bank balance. Certainly he has his feet more firmly planted on the ground than the average Sixties hippy – his principal USA tour costume was decorated with enormous dollar signs! – and he is never going to destroy his brain cells with hallucinogenic drugs. But what George has in common with the hippy is his preaching of a doctrine of non-violence and affection for all.

Culture Club are a reaction to the aggressive style of the punk bands which dominated English music in the late Seventies and early Eighties, but which were never accepted by the mass audience. Although he used to mix in the same social circles, Boy George is the antithesis of Johnny Rotten and has made him and his music seem dated.

RECENT HIGHS

By hanging loose, by saying 'Be what you are but don't push it', by not haranguing people (as Jon puts it) and by simply being relaxed, Culture Club have come as a relief to people in these hard times, a delightful fantasy into which they can escape.

Whether by accident or design, they have filled a gap which needed to be filled ... by being in the right place at the right time.

Culture Club, aided by the recently emerged power of video, have risen to wealth and international fame faster than anybody in the pop world ever has before. After all, for four London lads – sorry, Roy – London and *Essex* lads to have acquired over a million pounds each within eighteen months of going on the road can't be bad.

Boy George arrives at the Frank Sinatra concert with companion Jemma on 23rd September 1984, two days before his new single 'War Song' was released.

29

III
BLACK AND WHITE POP FOR CHILD EARS

'Culture Club is important to me. It's like a family.'

George has said that he has little in common with Roy and Mikey and that he feels closest to Jon – 'he's probably my best friend' – but the members of the band maintain that they are vital to his sense of well-being. George comes from a large, tough Catholic family and seems to need to work within a 'family context' for his creativity to sparkle. The four members of Culture Club depend upon each other and none of them would deny this.

Nevertheless, George is both the focal point of and the spokesman for the group; how could it be otherwise with his talent, peacock appearance and constant willingness to talk? George has always sought attention, from his earliest days at school right up to the present day. Now that he has got so much there's little chance of his letting it go. The papers and other media are constantly coming at him with questions and he is always good copy. He just needs to fly into London's Heathrow Airport to make the front pages of British national newspapers; if nothing else, it is certain that he will be wearing a spectacular new outfit.

Though George takes the lion's share of publicity and, by the strength of his personality and vision, dictates the image of the group, it would be quite wrong to think of the other members as being merely the springboard from which Boy George has launched his version of world conquest. They are by no means session musicians. Indeed the success enjoyed by Culture Club depends on the collective talent provided by each constituent part. Just as one could say that it is likely that Roy, Mikey and Jon would not have been as successful in a group without George, it is also probably true the other way round.

Though there has been jealousy within Culture Club over the exposure received by George, the problem has now been resolved, with the other Clubbers accepting how beneficial all that publicity has been for them. Each member seems to realise what he owes to the others, and George himself has always been keen to emphasise that the band is not 'Boy George And Culture Club' but 'Culture Club'. The real proof of this is the fact that all profits are shared equally; every advantage gained is pooled to the common band.

When the band was awarded a US Grammy for 'Best Song' in 1984, George was deeply angered that the television studio had provided only him with a seat on the set and that the other group members had to twiddle their thumbs in the wings well out of the limelight. When the camera passed over him on the set you could almost see him plotting revenge – and sure enough he was. When the time came for him to stand up and thank America for the award, he looked straight into the camera and, smiling wickedly, praised the nation 'for knowing a good drag queen when it saw one'. Tit for tat in

MAD ABOUT THE BOY

George's book, and doubtless the same mistake will never be made at a Grammy Award ceremony again.

George, of course, understands how such a mistake could be made and has pointed out, not unreasonably, that he was bound to be considered separately from the rest of the group. Even before he was Boy George he always stood out from the crowd, a fact which saw him turning up on TV programmes about 'how the young are dressed today', etc., or in the pages of magazines, the fashion pages usually. George also applied to be a presenter on Britain's Channel 4 TV pop show, The Tube; the fact that he was turned down has proved to be a blessing for everyone, but especially for him.

In the long run success has brought self-confidence to everyone in the group, and the personality clashes have died away, with Jon, Roy and Mikey (particularly Mikey and Ron) now much more able to cope with their positions in the group and their status as stars. Jon now has his own fan club, and all three are working hard at developing their own individual look, though these are intended to be complementary rather than competitive within the band. (Perhaps thankfully, there are no signs of Mikey returning to the semi-Mohican hairstyle of his early days in the band.)

If anyone can be called the founder of the group, it is probably Mikey. It was his persistence which probably brought Culture Club into existence. Still relatively young, he worked as a disc jockey at Club Sept in the West End of London, but he always felt more inclined to play his own rather than other people's music. One day someone left a bass guitar at his house in South London; he picked it up and started to play. Soon he had mastered some basic Bob Marley chords and he quickly decided he would love to be in a band.

However, Mikey had lots of other things to do and two children to look after, and consequently music took a back seat while he tried to make a living in all sorts of other ways, such as labouring or working in sound studios. Somehow he wasn't cut out for a nine-to-five existence.

On returning from Bristol, where he had gone to be with his wife Cleo and the kids for a while, he began to think seriously about how to form a band. He'd never been in one and had no clear idea at first how to go about

it. Early in 1981 he saw an article in *New Musical Express*, Britain's leading music paper, about the group BowWowWow. BowWowWow was managed at the time by Malcolm McLaren, the punk entrepreneur and Machiavellian media manipulator, who brought the world the Sex Pistols and then turned into a madcap rap artist himself. (Mr McLaren is one of the few people who could talk the hind legs off Boy George.) Lead singer of BowWowWow was Annabella Lu Win, a 14-year-old half-Burmese girl, whom McLaren discovered singing sweetly in his local dry cleaner's and put in the group he was forming. McLaren's idea was to sell the group on the idea of piracy and teenage (underage) sex. However, though moderately successful, the band never really sold huge amounts of records and McLaren decided they needed a new stimulus.

The article Mikey saw carried a picture of Annabella with BowWowWow's latest addition, a singer called Lieutenant Lush: an odd, almost ungainly, heavily made-up figure in cavalier lace, with clumps of hair tied fiercely into sheaves with little white bows. The article indicated that McLaren might be thinking of forming a new band around this singer, who, you must have guessed by now, was called George O'Dowd.

Mikey had friends who worked at McLaren's *avant-garde* King's Road clothes shop, World's End, which he ran with Vivienne Westwood (the woman who made punk and the pirate look run riot through the salons of *haute couture*). He phoned them up one day and asked whether there was any truth in the *New Musical Express* article, hoping that it might be his chance to get in at the start of a new group.

McLaren is a man with a thousand ideas running through his head at any given time, and it looked unlikely that he would ever follow the enquiry through, so Mikey forged ahead anyway and got to meet George at a London club called Planets, where George was disc jockey. The Boy was eager to be in a band of his own, because by now he'd left BowWowWow having failed to see eye to eye with McLaren. But McLaren had given George the taste for singing before the public and he knew he was cut out for a career of that kind.

George and Mikey decided to form a group virtually on the spot and immediately started to try and recruit a guitarist. However, this is more easily decided than done, and their total lack of experience made things worse. In the end, they recruited someone called John 'Suede' and a band was born, which they christened The Sex Gang Children (a name later bequeathed to another group). The members started rehearsing together, wrote a song and started to look for a drummer.

MAD ABOUT THE BOY

Since his squatting days at the famous house in Carburton Street which he shared with Marilyn, Jeremy Healey of Haysi Fantayzee and many other luminaries of the New Romantic scene, George had been friendly with Kirk Brandon (later the leader of Theatre Of Hate and Spear Of Destiny), and Kirk knew someone called Jon Moss, who had played drums with a number of groups, including The Damned and The Clash, and was reckoned to be good.

Jon met George for the first time in March 1981, after receiving a garbled summons over the phone. George was by this time a prince among *poseurs*. Although he strenuously kept aloof from any possibility of being parcelled up with the set dominated by Rusty Egan and Steve Strange, and the Blitz crowd, he was still well-known around town and considered a leading New Romantic, with his Gothick looks and caked make-up. On top of this, until recently he'd been Lieutenant Lush! Jon, who describes himself as a bit of a puritan and whose sense of style errs on the side of understatement, hated

BLACK AND WHITE POP FOR CHILD EARS

the Blitz scene and couldn't stand those who took part in it. Their first meeting didn't look promising.

Jon had of course seen George around – who hadn't? – but recalls that since George changed his look so often, he wasn't ever sure that the person he was seeing was the same person he saw before.

Previous sightings had prepared him for the shock of their meeting, and besides George had warned him over the phone that people thought he was 'over the top and far too effeminate'. Still, he wasn't quite prepared for the panting, fast-talking, painted creature in flowing robes, who pumped his hand the moment he walked into the room. Perhaps the greatest shock was that he liked the guy on sight. In fact, contrary to all expectations, they hit it off extremely well and this proved a blessing indeed for the future of Culture Club. If they had disliked each other, we might never have heard of either of them again.

Jon came into the band and provided not only a solid musical backbone but also organisational ability and hard-headed business sense. He was a man with experience of bands and he knew the pitfalls to avoid: many inexperienced bands spend years just paying back the record company's advance.

Jon immediately started to shape the group's career, soon bringing in Tony Gordon to look after the group's business affairs. He also began to act as the channel which brought order and flow to George's torrent of wild ideas. And from the outset he insisted on a couple of fundamental changes.

First the name Sex Gang Children had to go. Jon had had enough of Blitz style ideas; they were all too stark. He saw that something new was needed, for the group and for the pop scene in general. What could be better than breathing some warmth and light into the cobwebbed corridors of early Eighties London style? Jon wanted to make music with a wide appeal, for everyone ... not just the members of that clubbish elite of *poseurs*. He'd kicked

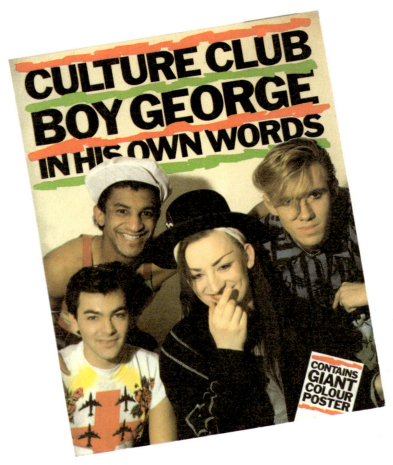

around – and been kicked around – in enough bands for far too long. Now he was in one where he had a creative say and it was like coming up for air. But the main thing was that he wanted to be in a band which sold records.

So the name Sex Gang Children gave way to Culture Club. The band say they chose the name for fun, but Jon said at the time that as the eventual members of the band were multicultural – he's Jewish, George is a Catholic from a London-Irish background, Mikey's black and Roy is a typical white working-class lad – it was a suitable title, and the band always intended to use the influences of lots of different cultures. Indeed the name says it all, as we now know.

At this time George had been in contact with Ashley Goodall of EMI, who'd been trying to persuade him to become a solo artist after the split with BowWowWow. George didn't really want this – as we've seen he prefers to have people around him – but EMI still let the band make a demo tape of the two new songs they'd written since Jon's arrival, EYES OF MEDUSA and I'M AN ANIMAL.

Making the tape was very good experience, but this work in the studio showed up the deficiencies of guitarist John 'Suede'. It seemed he had to go. Jon had, from the start, been wondering whether he was good enough, but he wasn't the first to act. After a month of dithering – it's never easy to sack someone, especially if you have worked closely with them – 'Suede' was asked to go ... and he went.

Once again therefore there was a gap in the Club and as everyone wanted to keep things moving, the pressure was on to find a replacement who would meet their high standard. He took some finding. Numerous auditions were held till one day a former insurance clerk who played guitar for an Essex band called Russian Bouquet ('disgustingly enough' – George!) turned up on the recommendation of somebody who knew George. His name was Roy Hay and he clicked immediately with the other three – impressing even the tough-minded Jon with his playing – and that was it, he was IN and Culture Club was complete.

Then began the sixteen months of sheer hard work that were to lead to DO YOU REALLY WANT TO HURT ME?

Rehearsals took place three or four times a week, always in the evenings, because they all had to work to make money during the day. It was especially hard on Roy, who was living some way out of London, near Basildon, a new town in Essex. After giving up his job in an insurance firm he'd trained as a hairdresser, and that was what he was doing when he joined. Life was tough; sometimes he spent all day cutting hair, then got on a train to London. On rehearsal nights, he often didn't get home until 1.30 in the morning.

What kept him and the others going through with something that they could easily have dropped at any time was the simple conviction that they were on the right track, that they had something going for them that was going to work. Even then they felt that what they were aiming for was something entirely new and that it had a good chance of taking the world by storm. Jon had persuaded George to discipline his writing, and made him aware of the importance of lyrical structure. Even more important, the voice was getting more assured day by day.

By October 1981 Culture Club were ready for their first concert, which took place at Crocs in Rayleigh, a small Essex town just north of Basildon. Crocs was a club Roy knew from his Russian Bouquet days, and the gig proved a fine test of character for the band. The clientele was, to say the least, a mixed bunch, with a fearsome reputation for rowdiness and an unwillingness to give a band an even break. The audience was mid-teens to early twenties, pretty rough, and its constitutent elements were rockabillies, skins and New Romantics all bundled together under the one roof.

But things worked out; Culture Club won them all over, which was an indication of how they were going to appeal to all sorts of people.

The band then went on to play concerts in Birmingham and London at the late end of 1981 - these were at The Holy City Zoo and Fooberts - before returning to do a Boxing Day performance at Crocs on Saturday 26th December.

This gig proved a turning point. By pure chance there was a man there called Danny Goodwin, who worked for a company called Virgin Music.

Goodwin was so impressed by their potential that he offered them the chance to make a demo tape for his company. This the band did, but the results were not what had been hoped for; it seems that George still sounded like too many other singers. Virgin were disappointed and so, for the moment, they and the band parted company again. But now Culture Club had to start looking for a record company on their own initiative - it was, after all, the next step in the process of becoming famous and successful.

A wearying trawl round all the record companies then began, but by now Jon's business instincts were reinforced by the acumen of a new manager in the shape of Tony Gordon.

Culture Club recorded WHITE BOY and I'M AFRAID OF ME on a demo for EMI again, but there was a difference in the music this time: the playing was stronger and George now had the confidence to use his own voice – he was beginning to sound like himself.

Eventually, they went back to Virgin. Despite the fact that Virgin weren't offering them as good a deal initially as they might have got elsewhere, they were offering them the freedom they needed to evolve their own style in their own time. 'I'd rather take 75 per cent of a million than 100 per cent of fuck all', said Jon. The potential that Danny Goodwin had sensed at the beginning of the previous year was coming out now, and Virgin responded by finally signing Culture Club.

The relationship between the youthful Virgin organisation and Culture Club has been very open-ended; it allowed the band to carve its own particular path through the rubble of the rock world. Virgin had faith in the Club and they were allowed to avoid standard gigs and go off on the then unfashionable tack of playing short tours.

Very cautiously, they augmented their core team of four with other musicians. The tours were well received but Culture Club weren't cutting a lot of ice in the charts. By September 1982, with two flops behind them, things were beginning to look a little shaky. Virgin kept backing them, but George and the others were beginning to have doubts.

Then came DO YOU REALLY WANT TO HURT ME?

'My last really outrageous thing was when I dressed up as Boadicea in red, white and blue and wore this absolutely huge hat which went right up to the sky and I stood outside Buckingham Palace during Trooping the Colour and everyone cheered and waved. After that I calmed down. I fell in love for three months and I just plaited the lot and put bells in it.'

IV
THE BOYS IN THE BAND

'The thing about a band, four people, is that you have to kind of delegate ideas and you also have to make things available for other people.'

Jon Moss is a lean, handsome, serious-faced man, who usually wears plain, figure-hugging clothes which offset his dark features. His face remains slightly scarred from a terrible car crash he had on New Year's Eve, 1977. His influence in Culture Club is not limited to drumming.

It was fortunate for Culture Club that two such natural opposites attracted, that Boy George and Jon Moss hit it off so well together; for Jon was, as I have said, the man with experience of the pop business, while George was the one who could provide the inspiration.

Jon is one of a new breed of pop musicians. Not only has he learnt the prime lessons of the twenty-five years during which pop music has been a cultural force, but his own experience of the underside of 'rock's rich tapestry' has kept his feet firmly on the ground and his eyes fixed on the goal of international success. After playing in a number of unnotable guitar thrash groups, Jon seems to have understood the perversity of appealing to only a narrow section of the public, when a more colourful approach can reach a much wider audience without compromising the band or its ideals. He points out that twenty years ago we knew nothing about what happened to pop stars when they grew old, because there weren't any who were! Now we do and impoverished pop stars are not a pretty sight. With this unhappy spectre at the backs of their minds, Culture Club are being directed in a businesslike and organised manner, with Moss the driving force.

But Culture Club are not just in it for the money. They have a strong set of beliefs, many of which are directed against traditional 'rockist values'. Jon believes it is vitally important – both in view of long-term success and in order to lay the basis for a powerful set of songs – for a group to project a message, which in Culture Club's case is described by Moss as 'the politics of living'.

The crucial part of the Culture Club manifesto is that there's no point in rejecting everything and throwing yourself into the world of drink and drugs. Culture Club's outlook is realistic and life-affirming: accept what you are and adapt to the circumstances. Boy George's make-up and clothes mark a gentle revolution against the standard of previous generations and their rigid conformities. While shocking at first, George's image now seems to blend comfortably into the average home whenever he appears on television, and people's attitudes have grown a degree or two more tolerant towards those who are unlike them. Barriers are slowly being broken down.

Nowadays the band are very confident. This is due to both the success of their records and the knowledge that success has been based on a firm foundation with their positive and open approach. The songs steer away from encouraging mindless rebellion in favour of a policy of questioning life in a positive way. A word Jon is fond of is 'radical', and his radical thinking is pure

common sense.

You could say that Culture Club are just saying, 'Look, the Emperor has no clothes on', and everybody's pleased and relieved because everybody's been trying to say just that for ages. Thinking of what George will look like in a few weeks' time, let alone years, makes the mind boggle; his is a continuous revolution.

One day Culture Club may toughen up their message but, meanwhile, partly as a reaction to the spitting Archdukes and hallucinating dowager duchesses of previous and more sordid generations of rock stars, the Club behave themselves in public – and show respect. They are aware of a responsibility to their public and have no intention of hurting either the numerous people from teenyboppers to grandmothers who buy their records, or, coincidentally, their record sales.

Jon has painted a chilling picture of the power of a group which can command and influence a vast army of millions of fans. Thousands hang on to Boy George's every word. What if Boy George had the same beliefs as Hitler? With such power comes responsibility and Culture Club are well aware of how important this is.

Jon has, as we have seen, been around for a while. He drummed for a band with the grotesque name of Eskimo Norbert, who played pop standards such as 'Johnny Be Good' and were never good enough to escape the icy wastes of pop failure. Then Jon strung along with the Clash, until their empty political posturing struck a raw nerve – in his neck! – and he left. Next came London, a shortlived escapade in the history of rock, and this was followed by a brief tour of duty with The Damned, whose battle-scarred members recently called it a day and have resigned themselves to more graceful middle age. These are just a few of his favourite former groups and you can imagine what the rest were like. To cut a long story short, Jon knows the scene, and that is why he thought shifting the said scene could only be a good thing.

One incident stands out particularly. When Jon had his car crash on New Year's Eve 1977, apparently no one in The Damned, his group at the time, came to see him in hospital. However, not everyone in pop is uncaring, and The Stranglers, who Jon once played support to, did their grape-carrying bit and popped by to aid his convalescence. Happily Jon recovered completely.

Jon developed his perception of the music business and realised there was a gap in the pop jungle which needed to be filled. With Jon acting as guide, Culture Club filed past the lotus-bearing reps of the record companies, on whose altars all too many ignorant young pop starlets have been slaughtered after acquiescence that would put a sacrificial lamb to shame. Through Jon's astuteness, Culture Club have made the system work for them – not least by opting for a contract with Virgin, the highly successful youth-oriented British multi-media entertainments company founded and headed by Richard Branson.

Jon argues that a revolution has been brought about by Culture Club and that this is based on a widening of the parameters of tolerance, the kind of revolution that Jon favours. Effectively, his argument runs along lines that any revolutionary change for the better in life must come from within – within a person, within a society; put otherwise, non-violently. You can persuade, but not bludgeon. Persuasion is the thing that works. Simply, indirectly, by example, Culture Club have exercised a subtle subversion of the norm.

Jon Moss was born in Wandsworth, South London, on 11th September 1957, the son of a Jewish girl from the North of England and a professional violinist. He was adopted by a Jewish couple and brought up within that culture, although he went to Church of England schools. His background is comfortable middle-class, and he had what is called 'a good education'. Small for his age, he was encouraged to take up boxing by his

father, Lionel, so that he would be able to defend himself in every situation. He was keen on sport, and developed into a good boxer, but gave it up when he was fifteen because he didn't like the effect the sport had on others who had stayed with it. Being punched in the head doesn't do your brain cells much good. Meanwhile he'd developed another interest: music. Perhaps he inherited this passion from his true father, the violinist. Starting with the piano, he went on to drums at about the age of fourteen. He practised regularly with his brother David and a friend called Nick Feldman, who is now a member of Wang Chung.

School over (he left with A levels in English, Politics and History) he did a short stint in his adoptive father's business in the clothing industry before drifting through a variety of shortlived jobs as a cake salesman (total sales, zero), a printer and a van driver.

Luck went against Jon on his first forays into the music business, but finally he got a foot in the door when he set up a band with Nick Feldman. They called it Phone Bone Boulevard and set off down the path to fame and fortune; unfortunately this proved badly signposted, and they had insufficient local knowledge to get anywhere. Phone Bone Boulevard fell apart and was succeeded by years of applying for jobs advertised in the music press, and moving from group to group to group. In the course of his travels, Jon was once voted 'the prettiest punk' in a fanzine, which reminds you that he's changed his image a lot since then! His name was steadily getting around and one day the phone rang. On the line was a gabbling and garrulous friend of Kirk Brandon called George O'Dowd.

Jon isn't the only sportsman on the team. George himself was encouraged to box by his own father as a kid and it is rumoured by some that he still packs quite a punch, belying his image. Mikey Craig, too, was excellent at football at school and was approached for trials by Brentford and Fulham football clubs. His parents, though, put a stop to anything like that. They wanted him to get some academic qualifications under his belt first.

Mikey didn't have too promising a start to his musical career either. His father had been a singer in Jamaica before the war, and later as well, when he settled in England. He thus knew the uncertain kind of profession music could be, and family ambitions for Mikey were fixed on a secure and respectably job: a lawyer or a doctor son would have been fine. But this didn't mean to say that Mikey's interest in music was discouraged. On the contrary, he grew up with music all around him.

To put it mildly, Mikey has had a busy span of years. Born in Hammersmith on 15th February 1960, he's packed more into his life so far than most people could manage in a whole series of reincarnations. When he

THE BOYS IN THE BAND

was young and still in his teens he became romantically involved with a girl called Cleo, the daughter of women's rights campaigner Erin Pizzey. As time went on, they moved into a flat together and by the time Mikey was eighteen, he was the father of two beautiful children, son Kito and daughter Amber.

Money was short. And with two children to support, Mikey took on a number of tough jobs, including roadbuilding, to earn it. Despite a continuing reputation for being lazy, he eventually found a job in a sound studio as a tape editor. Being good at this, he intended to stay on ... but his interest in making his own music was stronger than ever and in his spare time he was teaching himself bass guitar.

His relationship with Cleo was souring, but his devotion to her and the children was never in doubt; when she moved to Bristol he followed, and it was there that he first decided to form his own band. Since Bristol didn't seem to him the place to do it, he persuaded Cleo to move back to London with him about the middle of 1980.

Mikey's infectious smile, which seems irrepressible even in the most serious Culture Club photograph, indicates a sunny personality, and he must have needed it to get through the following months. But Mikey was determined, and when he opened the *New Musical Express* early in 1981 and saw that article about BowWowWow, with the young Annabel Lu Win posing, as we have seen, next to the ungainly and improbable military Lieutenant Lush, he reached for the telephone.

Mikey's relationship with Cleo was foundering, and when Erin Pizzey moved to Santa Fé in New Mexico a few months later Cleo went too, taking Kito and Amber with her. At least they are still in good terms, and Mikey visits his children as often as he can, which is a lot more often than would have been the case if Culture Club had not been successful.

When the Pizzeys left for New Mexico, Cleo's younger brother Amos also ended his association with Culture Club. As Captain Crucial he had guested on the song LOVE TWIST, demonstrating astounding vocal talents for a fourteen-year-old. But his introduction to the band hadn't met with unanimous approval at first. Roy Hay was dead against it – until he heard the result.

Roy is the youngest member of the Club (he's almost two months younger than George) and he was also the last to join. Until recently he's been labelled as the 'shy one', at least in public, and he is also the one most involved with the creation of the music itself. He tends to steer clear of the publicity generated by the band, and is quite happy to leave that side of things to George.

> *'People tend to associate me with the clubs and the discos but my idea of a really good time is a quiet dinner with a friend in a good restaurant.'*

But as the group develops, so he is changing with it, and finding the confidence for the evolution of his image, as we'll see later. He's always had strong opinions within the band, though some of these opinions have not been popular: when George first presented the band with the lyrics of KARMA CHAMELEON, Roy thought the whole idea so dreadful that they should immediately junk it!

Son of a docker, Roy was born in the seaside town of Southend, Essex, which is famous for having the longest pier in the world. Most of his life has been spent in the Essex commuter belt beside Basildon New Town.

Roy is slim, fair-haired, quiet and not the least bit unassuming. He demands a lot from everybody. He's not easily fazed either and, like the rest of the band, takes a positive approach to life, especially where the music is concerned. Hooked on the piano as a child, he's always been obsessed with music. His early influences were groups like Yes, Led Zeppelin and Genesis and since he picked up his first guitar at the age of fifteen, learning all the solos

he could from his records, he has hardly put it down for any length of time.

His first job was with a London insurance company and he had no intention of going into pop music professionally. However, during his three years as an insurance clerk he became friends with one Keith Giddons. Keith used to shop at a place called Street Theatre, where someone called George O'Dowd was working at the time . . .

But all that came later. Before it happened Roy had given up the doubtless fascinating world of insurance and turned to hairdressing as a replacement. He remembers enjoying his work in the salon (he worked there during the early days of Culture Club), but his real interest lay in music. He was still playing piano and guitar (then as now, since he plays lead guitar and keyboard with Culture Club), and in his attempts to teach himself more about musical structure he even borrowed a set of drums to lay down a beat and produced a home-made demo tape.

His musical career, which he was still pursuing as a sideline, was given a boost when he met and fell in love with a girl called Alison Green at Crocs Night Club. Her brother had a band called Russian Bouquet, and they needed a guitarist. That association didn't last long, because Roy was soon to audition for Culture Club, but the one with Alison did; in fact, he married her on 24th December 1982 – just two months after DO YOU REALLY WANT TO HURT ME? went to Number One in the UK charts and the band's fame was assured.

But there have been bad moments for the band. Halfway through the USA tour in September 1983, Boy George angrily put paid to rumours that Culture Club were going to split up. This was at the time when it was rumoured that the other boys in the band had begun to feel that they were becoming a glorified backing group for Boy George. Things weren't helped by the fact that George himself was under a great deal of strain at the time. The situation had come about owing to the clash of four strong personalities, all working closely together in the constant glare of publicity and in the face of vicious rumours stirred up by the press. However, this announcement saw the end of their worst period together, and the difficulties have now been largely resolved.

Now, just as each member takes an equal amount out of the group (each one is a millionaire in his own right and they have organised their collective finances so that they each receive about £1,000 a month in salary) so each member is expected to put an equal amount of effort in. It is a policy which has paid dividends. The result is that each member of the group is now emerging as an individual – and instead of all the attention falling on George, each one is beginning to enjoy his share of the limelight, as well as the money.

'All I'm doing is making things that would have been outrageous ten years ago normal. Britain is well known for its eccentrics, and I just consider myself to be one of them. I don't worry what people say. I usually frighten them more than they frighten me. But if someone was to hit me, I would certainly hit back. What I really like are fat women at bus-stops. They aren't worried about the way I look, and simply say "Hello love, I've seen you on telly loads of times".'

V

SCHOOL, SEX AND STYLE

*'It's difficult for people to understand me. Although I look obvious
there's much more to me than people see.'*

It's dark in the hall of heroes at Madame Tussaud's and the figures are dramatically spotlit. George is on his own, sitting on a Japanese-style plinth in front of an illuminated panel that could have come out of a painting by Mondrian.

Just along from George is one of his heroes, David Bowie, the man who brought pop music into the Seventies and who remains a leading light in the Eighties. Bowie is a culture chameleon and has consciously cultivated a constantly evolving image to keep well ahead of the field. George fell under Bowie's influence in the early Seventies, when the latter was going on stage as Ziggy Stardust, and since then has been obsessed with the idea of image and style. To understand George's need for dressing up it is probably necessary to go back in time, to his family and the circumstances of his childhood.

Boy George was born George Alan O'Dowd on 14th June 1961 in the south London borough of Eltham. His father is a builder and his mother works part-time in an old people's home. Their family, as one would expect of Irish Catholics, is a large one: George is the third of six children – five boys and a girl – and when he was young, the small council house occupied by the O'Dowds was further crowded by two Alsatian dogs.

Life was not easy in this overcrowded environment. Money was short and George's father, Jerry, was preoccupied with keeping his large family fed as he built up his own business after leaving the army. There was little time for him to give his children the affection they each needed, besides the fact that he usually got home exhausted from work.

Although he took the ten-year-old George boxing at a club in Eltham, where the boy turned out to be 'very handy with his fists', Jerry O'Dowd tended to be remote and tough rather than loving. The house in Joan Crescent was too small for the family and there was a great deal of tension. George's eldest brother, Richard, who went through a phase of skinhead rebellion, had such a row with his mother that he left home and didn't return for seven years.

The problems are in the past now, and there is a close family feeling in the O'Dowd household (George is still very loyal and fiercely loving to his parents), but this didn't come about before father and son had had a massive battle which culminated in George locking himself in the bathroom, and Jerry smashing the door down. This was when George was 14. After escaping from

the avenging figure of his father, George ran away from home for two weeks to stay with a friend's parents. He only returned after a phone call from his parents. 'From then on it was fine. My dad changed completely. Now he's brilliant!'

If the dressing up started as a means of gaining more of his parents' attention ('I felt that my mother and father didn't show any affection towards me. And all the time that was what I wanted. I wanted to kiss my father. I wanted affection'), it succeeded but also left them bewildered. There didn't seem to be much they could do about their son's peculiar 'hobby', and George managed to persuade them to let him go his own way.

Other threats to self-expression loomed large, however. There was school for a start, and this presented great difficulties to the boy whose main desire was not to conform.

At the time, Eltham Green Comprehensive was run by Peter Dawson, a headmaster who had been able in a relatively short time to bring a tough school to heel by introducing a rule of strict discipline. Naturally George did not see eye to eye with the school authorities and this educational atmosphere was hardly the place for a pupil such as he to flourish. But nothing deterred him from dressing flamboyantly, not even the mockery of his fellow students. 'The word "misfit" could have been coined for George O'Dowd,' says Peter Dawson. 'He did not fit in and he did not want to fit in.'

In the end, George was relegated from the classroom to the school's 'sanctuary unit' at the top of the building. This was known as *The Greenhouse* and there George found himself in the company of other incurables and reprobates, as well as the school psychiatrist, who seems to have joined George in a series of battles of will which only ended when George ditched formal education for the big, wide world outside.

Unprepared to do the work the school set him, George had been skipping school more and more often. And when he did turn up, he had become more and more insolent and uncooperative. On 29th September 1976, Mr and Mrs O'Dowd received a letter suspending their son from school and, even though George accompanied his mother for a meeting with headmaster Dawson, no compromise could be reached and George left with a dishonourable discharge.

Since George's rise to fame, his conduct and the treatment meted out to him by the school have been the subject of much discussion in the press – including *The Times Educational Supplement*, where Dawson's draconian methods came in for criticism. The conclusion reached by those involved in the debate was that, for whatever reasons, George, an intelligent and imaginative boy, was unable to express himself at school and received no

SCHOOL, SEX AND STYLE

encouragement to pursue his obvious artistic interests there. In fairness to the teachers, though, it should be said that George's stubbornness made him very hard to handle. 'I hated school ... they made fun of my high voice and the way I looked. But it made me a stronger person.'

George isn't at all proud of his school record, and nowadays is keen to emphasise that he thinks people should make the most of their education. Eltham Green Comprehensive was a waste of time for George, a place where he took the role of jester and rebel. It was only when he left that he could begin his proper education.

George has always been deliberately evasive about his sex life. Sometimes it's girls, sometimes it's boys, and sometimes it isn't there at all. Keeping people guessing is good for keeping people interested, but after all, as he himself says, what's really important is his music, not what he does, or doesn't do, between the sheets.

As an adolescent, George had no shortage of girlfriends. Romantically, the most important was Shelley Hughes, over whom the Boy quite lost his head. As an in-influence though, George's most significant girlfriend was Tracey Birch. When he met her in the spring of 1975, he was already well into his David Bowie look, but by the time he returned to school at the end of the summer holidays that year, his former image seemed tame by comparison with what was a stunning new look. Tracey had encouraged him to experiment; the result was flaming orange hair (poor camouflage for a frequent truant), tight drainpipe trousers, orange socks, plastic sandals and a cut-down tie worn over a collarless shirt.

As for the actual relationship with Tracey, she says it was strictly platonic and that they were more like brother and sister than sweethearts. She remembers too that he scored a big hit with her mum with his politeness and the fact that he always offered to do the washing up; quite a contrast to his disruptive behaviour at school. Apparently Tracey's mum still thinks fondly of George: 'She still cries when she sees him on Top Of The Pops.'

It was about this time, when he was just fifteen, that George started going out to gay clubs – partly because that was the only club scene where anything interesting was going on and partly also because his appearance was acceptable among the gay community.

Although there were precedents in the pop world, such as Bowie or Elton John, George's appearance outdid almost anyone else's in those days and could be a problem. In the gay clubs he could dress as he wanted without fear of violence and could therefore pursue his research into the farthest reaches of dressing up (sometimes dressing down) in the most absurd bits and pieces. He began speeding up the turnover of images, getting the clothes he needed from market stalls, Oxfam shops, jumble sales and his mother's pile of throwaways. Leaving school meant he could launch himself on the London scene in earnest, taking various odd jobs to support his 'clothes habit' and still living with his parents – in the larger house in Shooter's Hill which the council had by now mercifully provided.

This was a time when all sorts of styles were shooting off in all sorts of directions, with punk, Forties to Sixties revivals and variations, and the beginnings of the New Romantic look as the main streams. In such a watershed it's no wonder that George isn't the only one to emerge as a new light on the fashion scene. Early friends and influencers included Philip Sallon, Martin Degville and Stephen Linard (now a successful designer in Tokyo); not to mention the King of Camden Palace, Welsh import Steve Strange.

The newspapers and magazines of Britain soon caught on to George and his appearance. When he first started modelling *avant-garde* fashions and became a cult figure on the club circuit, he was much in demand by editors on the lookout for bizarre items to pep up their columns. As soon as his picture was published, the text of any accompanying piece could be relied on to concentrate on how extraordinary he looked, and then to dwell on whether he was a normal girl or an abnormal boy. The term 'cross-dressing' was eventually invented to cover his chosen mode of attire.

In fact, George insists that his clothes are *not* women's clothes – they don't even button right-over-left – and that underneath them he wears Y-Fronts, as he's always at pains to point out. Nor is he particularly feminine. He wears make-up because he likes it and because he thinks it makes him look better: he doesn't wear it to look like a woman.

In a famous quote, he described himself as a 'pouf with muscles' but he was sending himself (and his interviewer) up at the time; just as he was at the Grammy Award when he described himself as a drag queen. The truth is that George has kept the world guessing and wrongfooted the media with a variety of disarming replies to their questions. 'Gay, hetero or bi?' was the question posed by one member of the press and George replied 'Does it matter?' Finally they decided that George was having an affair with Jon Moss and there are plenty of photos of Jon being kissed on the lips by the Boy, which might seem to back up such a suggestion. However, George always has a good laugh when any of this is suggested, and one can assume that if he is having an affair with someone it will be shielded from the public gaze.

If the subject of sex brings out mischievous wit in George, there is no doubt about his attitude to love, and to any loving relationship between two people. George knows that love is the most important thing in life and it is what everybody needs to give and to get. Without it, sex is ultimately a waste of time. George loathes the idea of sleeping around and would never consider sleeping with one of his fans – ever practical, he points out the damage that the discovery of such a thing would do to his popularity. It may have helped the Rolling Stones in their career, but it wouldn't help George or Culture Club.

George says that love is a private thing, not to be sold to the papers for public consumption. He also says the people he has loved will always be important to him and that he will never sell them out. This sense of morality seems to have been brought home to his fans and on the 1984 tour of America, one of them enthused, 'Boy has a lot of morals and standards. He doesn't even have a sex life. He's a very good person.'

It is unlikely, however, that George actually considers sex to be bad and he has certainly had a number of lovers. He says he has never been the one to end any of his relationships and that this is due to his sense of responsibility

to his partner. As for his ambivalent sexuality, it is something that seems to emerge particularly strongly in still photographs but is less apparent when he is moving on stage. If anything, his sexuality is understated in his stage performance and a flaunting of this would, coming from the Boy, seem undignified or at the very least inappropriate. And he knows it.

When still living at home, an ordinary working-class London lad, he used to catch the 122 bus back home after his nights on the tiles. To earn money for his nightclubbing, he worked at a clothes shop called Shades in the Chelsea Antique Market and then later moved on to a job as shelf-filler at Tesco's supermarket. Tesco's and George only enjoyed each other's company for a week, which just gave him time to provoke the management with his dress sense and then get sacked for wearing their carrier bags to go about his tasks of lining up tins on the shelves and piling packets in the freezer.

At this time, he was spending a lot of time in clubs. Near where he lived, in Bexleyheath, was the Black Prince and he used to go there when he wasn't in town. Up in town, it was Shaguaramas, Louise's and The Global Village. But it was at Bangs that he first encountered the outrageous Philip Sallon, a man who favours *much* more bizarre clothing than George. For a moment he was upstaged and nonplussed, but he soon got over this and the two became firm friends, despite the occasional and gleefully recorded screaming match.

George had found a soulmate and it was marvellous to discover there were other people in the world who enjoyed doing what he did. This gave

SCHOOL, SEX AND STYLE

George a new confidence.

In 1976 George moved up to Birmingham and shared a flat with hairdresser and clothes designer Martin Degville. The move was like a breath of fresh air for him and he really enjoyed living up there. He and Martin ran a clothes stall in the Oasis Market and sought to outdo and outdress each other on their frequent forays into the city's nightlife. Within a year, though, George had had his fill of Birmingham and returned to London, which offered more scope in the long run for someone with his talents.

A club called Billy's was just starting up at the time, masterminded by Steve Strange and his partner Rusty Egan. There were regular Bowie nights, when the music played was predominantly Bowie's and where people were encouraged to dress up glamorously and dance till dawn. The recession was just hitting England and in part the club provided a cheap means for its members to forget about the boredom and poverty of their everyday lives and become stars within the club scene. You didn't need money ... all you needed was style and the courage to carry it off.

The scene began to grow and grow and George became one of its most prominent figures. In 1980 the crowd moved to the Blitz, a club in London's Covent Garden district, and it was there that the New Romantics, or Blitz kids, mustered and began what was to be a very successful assault on the world of fashion and music. Soon the newspapers were carrying reports on what they saw as a decadent and weird new subculture. This proved, as so often, to be a prelude to the Blitz look catching on with the public.

People seemed to want to take pictures of George and plaster them all over their pages, but it was scarcely making him money, so he signed on at the Peter Benison model agency, which was at that time building up a 'new look' file to reflect the anticipated fashions in advertising and magazines. George became a 'face' in stylish magazines. He gave an interview to *Kicks*, a short-lived teen mag, then posed for British Airways ads and The Trustee Savings Bank (along with many of his friends). At a Spandau Ballet concert (Spandau also emerged from the Blitz scene), he charged photographers 50 pence per pose. At other times he modelled Melissa Caplan's clothes and did nifty turns up the catwalk.

George had by now become a full-blown socialite and London was undergoing a revolution, in which the New Romantics were the advance guards. There were lots of parties to go to – more accurately to gatecrash – and premieres. No one questioned the outlandishly dressed figure George cut; after all looking like

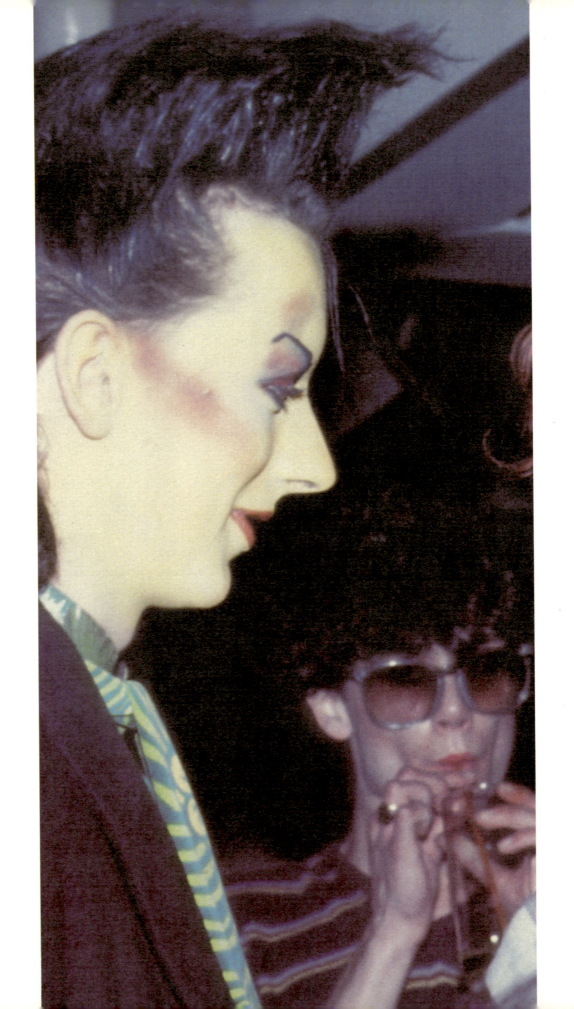

he did it didn't seem as if he was sneaking in. At the premiere of 'Breaking Glass', a film starring Hazel O'Connor, George and his entourage had to hide in the cinema lavatories when they heard they were to be thrown out.

By now George was living in a squat in the West End of London – in Carburton Street, off Great Portland Street and just south of Regent's Park. The huge house is gone now, demolished to make way for new offices, and it is a pity, since if it were still standing it would one day carry a collection of blue plaques to commemorate those famous people who once lived there.

Its crumbling bulk housed some of the most talented people in London, a kind of slum aristocracy of the fashion world. Occupants included the now famous milliner Stephen Jones (who not only makes hats for Boy George and Alannah Currie of The Thompson Twins, but also these days for the Princess of Wales), designer Melissa Caplan, Jeremy Healey (ex-Haysi Fantayzee and currently an artful dodger of the Eighties club scene) and singer Marilyn, whose on/off affair/friendship with Boy George has received so much publicity.

'I've never met anyone who taught me anything . . . I learnt everything I know from the street.'

The squat had a shifting population whose main purposes were to infiltrate the existing fashionable scene, and to create its own. George himself occupied the entire second floor and filled this with his collection of dolls and the bizarre trappings of his chosen way of life. The drab surroundings – bare floorboards, makeshift furniture, no hot water and only the one cold tap in the basement – were given colour and brought to life by the glittering ideas and dress of the occupants. In short it was an exciting place to live, where the collective inspiration and reforming zeal of each member of the household transcended the squalor and poverty of the surroundings.

Living with such energetic and exotic people, George grew ambitious. It wasn't enough to be a *poseur*, however much attention it could gain you. He saw that other people had plans that could get them somewhere in life and began looking into one of his own. He'd always been a good singer and had even performed at parties, generally camping it up with old pop songs and bizarre party pieces.

While still on the books of the Peter Benison agency, he started to write lyrics – he'd enjoyed creative writing at school but never followed it up –

and began keeping an eye out for opportunities in the music business. Luck has never been far from George's elbow, and it so happened that a girl called Gabriella, who handled his bookings at the agency, had a friend called Matthew Ashman, who was guitarist with BowWowWow. Malcolm McLaren was having trouble with the band's singer at the time, so George went along to help out and a career in music began.

But there was a gap between George's shortlived Lieutenant Lush period and the start of Culture Club. After he got out of BowWowWow and away from McLaren, George's prowess as a stylist led him into work as a dresser on the Royal Shakespeare's production of 'Naked Robots', a play which required a genuine punk look from its wardrobe department. He got the costumes he needed from a shop in Newburgh Street (just behind Carnaby Street in Soho) called Street Theatre. He got the costumes free, which delighted the RSC, in return for a plug for the shop in the programme. Peter Small, the shop's proprietor, liked George's sense of style enough to offer him a job as a window-dresser after his stint at the RSC was over. This was to have important consequences.

While George was dressing windows in Street Theatre and in The Regal, Small's other shop across the road which specialised in Sixties revival clothes, he met a designer called Sue Clowes. Her speciality was textile designs and these clicked with George immediately. Inspired, he got together with her to work out a range of clothing using her prints. With Small's backing they set up a shop called The Foundry in nearby Ganton Street and started to sell clothes which were a radical departure from those then in fashion. Culture Club's initial image was completely based on Foundrywear. Photographs from 1982 and early 1983 show the band dressed in these colourful clothes, and they provided them with an excellent start in the publicity stakes. The clothes are bright and beautifully printed with an eclectic blend of symbols gathered from each and every source, religious, tribal and technological, often on a white background. The Sue Clowes look was stunning with its combinations of crucifixes, Star of David motifs, four-engined plane shapes, red and green roses, and blue hearts impaled on daggers or a St George's Cross. The designs were for shirts, tank tops, T-shirts and trousers.

One of the symbols that figured largely in the early days of Culture Club was the Star of David. George claimed to have dropped it after it was suggested that some Jews had objected to its use in what they saw as a frivolous context. It does still appear from time to time, but the image the group presents today is a new one. Foundrywear has given way to Common Currency.

'A lot of people want to be like David Bowie. I don't.
I think he's had it really. I think he's great, brilliant,
but he's just there, like Harrods or Frank Sinatra.'

VI

MAD ABOUT THE BOY

'My personality is what sold me.'

The squats, and life around the squats, was a boom time for George. He was heavily into nightclubbing and was regularly to be found at Heaven, Le Beat Route, Visuals or the Roxy as well as the Blitz. This circuit of clubs was helpful in establishing a network of contacts for him as well as inspiring him with ideas and experiences. It also gave him the chance to continue experimenting with his costumes and his expertise in this area was increasing all the time.

George has had very little formal education. He once said he had only ever finished one book in his whole life, Tallulah Bankhead's autobiography, 'Tallulah Darling'. Where George looked for his education was out on the streets and in the clubs of London. His appearance often got him into trouble. 'Everybody was dressing up, and suddenly it was punk rock. Suddenly you started getting punched in the mouth. Everywhere you went, you got hit.'

It was a tough school he chose and maybe one which has given him the strength to cope with eventual success. A comparison has been made between George and Quentin Crisp, and both are very strong-minded. Crisp used to dress outrageously and frequent illicit homosexual haunts back in the days when homosexuality was against the law. Crisp flaunted his gay appearance and would often be attacked for it. Sometimes he could disarm would-be assailants by saying 'I seem to have upset people somehow', but more often than not he had to bear the brunt of people's intolerance.

George is certainly not afraid to stick up for himself either, and not just with words. After all, he is round about six foot tall and has learnt the rudiments of boxing from his father. 'A lot of people might think I'm a wimp but when I punch them in the mouth, they quickly learn the error of their ways!'

Under the flowing robes, there is a physique which has been described as chunky, although recently it does appear that George may have been putting on weight. His clothes have remained baggy so it's hard to tell. Sue Clowes designs have gone – the roses and the planes replaced by multicoloured numbers and dollar signs or polemical slogans such as 'Worldwide Nuclear Ban Now' – but the new outfits remain generously cut. 'People don't know whether it's muscles or fat under these clothes.'

As George himself has pointed out, his clothes can hide a multitude of sins. Many fans have adopted this clothing (and strategem) for disguising faults in their appearance. With clothes such as these, you can be comfortable and forget the 'body fascism' of the fashion world. Big clothes and heavy make-up are perfect cover.

George is surprisingly forthright about his physical deficiencies: viewed from certain angles, he has a double chin; he gets spots just like everybody else; he loathes organised exercise and sports. While he might seem a very exotic

MAD ABOUT THE BOY

creature at first sight, it may be that people actually like him for being so like they themselves are.

George knows, though, that his appearance is vitally important and is very careful about it. When he came back from his holiday in Jamaica with Marilyn in July 1984, with his new blond, tufty-bearded look, the fans' cheers turned to jeers ... he had disturbed their illusions about the Boy George image.

A glimpse of the inner Boy is perhaps harder to come by. George's tastes in music run from Motown to musicals, taking in many things along the way. George is not elitist or snobbish, and his favourite bands include Madness, Musical Youth, Yazoo, BowWowWow, Depeche Mode and Shalamar. Individual singers he likes are: Ella Fitzgerald, Dolly Parton, Cliff Richard (whom he admires for keeping his private life private), Michael Jackson, Gladys Knight and Tom Jones.

These lists omit his two great heroes. One, as I have said before, is David Bowie, whom George has described as 'perfect' (and George has a complete set of his albums). The other is Marc Bolan, who tragically died in a car accident a few years ago. George wanted to have corkscrew hair like Bolan's but his parents drew the line at this.

His all-time favourite list of records is very catholic and he seems to be open to all kinds of influences. Included are Blue Mink's MELTING POT, Tom Jones's IT'S NOT UNUSUAL, Gene Pitney's 24 HOURS FROM TULSA; JOLENE by Dolly Parton, and THE WAY WE WERE by Gladys Knight and the Pips.

Though he claims to have finished only one book in his life, his favourite reading in fact includes 'The Hobbit', 'Stig Of The Dump' and Lewis Carroll's classic 'Alice in Wonderland'.

When it comes to TV, George likes Top Of The Pops and goes utterly gaga over Coronation Street, which he follows as closely as any fan could ever follow Culture Club. His favourite character in this superior soap opera is Bet Lynch, the barmaid at The Rover's Return.

George's favourite pastime is going round art galleries and, in a recent interview, he was asked if he'd ever grow up to be Man George. 'Man Ray', he replied, naming one of the leading Surrealist artists and a man who may have shared some of George's views on life, for he said: 'Ever since our love for machines replaced the love we used to have for our fellow man, catastrophes proceed to increase.' And Man Ray and Boy George have something else in common: they've both had

their portraits drawn by David Hockney.

George has strong views on people. Among his favourites he lists his mum and dad (good boy), Jon Moss and Culture Club's manager, Tony Gordon. Another close friend is Kate Garner, who used to be in Haysi Fantayzee. He's also said that he adores Elizabeth Taylor and Culture Club's big-voiced backing singer, Helen Terry. 'I like Elizabeth Taylor's attitude. She's the only woman in Hollywood who doesn't care, and hasn't had a face-lift. That's something I really admire.'

As for the Royal Family, George says he likes Princess Anne 'because she's a bit like me – she swears at photographers!' – a reference to one famous occassion at London's Heathrow Airport in August 1983. But then adds, 'My favourite member of the Royal Family has to be Princess Diana because she's like me ... a workaholic. I really believe she has saved the Royal Family.'

He shows great respect too to his own family these days. He says that for him charity begins at home, and so mother and father, brothers Richard, Keith, Gerald and David and sister Siobhan will benefit from his good fortune. This unassuming, working-class Irish Catholic family ('My family is pretty orthodox. They've got a picture of the Pope in the hall') is proud of George's enormous success, and proud to retain their own independence of it. George has always – since the famous row which caused him to leave home when he was fourteen – been the loving son he wanted to be from the start. When his father had a heart attack, George was busy working and his mother, Diana, didn't tell him until Jerry was off the danger list. The thought that he hadn't known hurt George deeply. 'I'm generous to my family although I'd never just give my parents money. You take away people's dignity like that. You can do anything you want in life, but you have to give those around you dignity.'

As George's career took off, he learnt to handle the press. At first, journalists tended to sneer about his appearance, then they became suspicious of his charm as they realised that he was here to stay. Finally, they succumbed and became its victims; how can you keep condemning someone who always exhibits good humour and grace?

Influential columnist Marje Proops of *The Daily Mirror* gave him the final seal of approval in May 1984, when she wrote an article on how he'd won her over completely. This accolade from the best popular British newspaper ties in with George's view of himself – a working-class kid playing to a working-class audience. 'I've always respected my audience. I've always said they are a very

working-class audience, a very *TV Times* audience!'

Despite his vast collection of dolls and his alluring looks, Boy George comes across as straightforward to the point of brashness, something he may have inherited from his father. His handshake is firm and his manner is polite in public, but apparently 'offstage' he can be quite bitchy; 'off camera' his tongue can sting like a whip. It's easy to see that he is very determined to succeed and may even fit the description of 'workaholic'; at any rate he likes things to be perfect. But his feet are firmly planted in reality ... don't be fooled by his appearance.

He also insists on his 'ordinariness'. 'No one's mum need worry too much about Boy George.' In fact, he says he has never cultivated a mysterious image and that if people are intrigued by him and his apparent ambiguities then it is not the result of any contrivance on his part. His skill as a self-promoter lies in his ability to hold out on the press and he utilises the paradox of his appearance and his personality to the full. He shocks only by his appearance and that is enough to keep him in the public eye. 'I'm not an immoral person. Inside, I'm a rather conservative, moral, old-fashioned soul. I'm not a transvestite. I'm not promiscuous. I don't sleep with my fans and I certainly don't go in for orgies. I never touch drugs and I hardly drink. It all sounds rather boring, doesn't it?' Does it? It sounds more as if, with a new generation, the pendulum of reaction swings back again. After all, when The Beatles and The Rolling Stones were up there ringing the bells, George was about 4 years old.

He's a fluent talker, though sometimes the words get ahead of the ideas and trip them up. It seems as if he can't wait to tell you his ideas and opinions. George may not have been a success at school but no one could accuse him of being stupid.

'I feel sorry for all the people who laugh at me. The most abnormal thing in the world is to try and look like everyone else.'

When he was voted best Male *and* Female vocalist in a readers' poll in a popular music paper he didn't mind at all, though jokes like this about him have grown rather tired. He has a gift for fielding everything that is thrown at him, with apparent good will – in public at least – and seems always able to give as good as he gets. With his gift of mimicry, he is well capable of taking the mickey out of anyone who gets on the wrong side of him. He can make friends

speechless with laughter when he embarks on one of his famous bitching sessions, and it is thought best never to make yourself the butt of one of these.

One of the things you notice about Boy George is that he talks about himself a great deal of the time. What would in many other people be a terribly dull habit is in fact forgivable, since in this case the subject is so fascinating. George is never boring.

Perhaps, if there is one thing which George has proved, it is that you don't have to be sexy to succeed in pop music. Time and again, he has made the statement that he isn't a physical person and that he just isn't sexy. He has compared his own physical attributes to those of Simon Le Bon and found them wanting, but he is so disarming in this revelation that he makes it seem as if it is Le Bon who is really missing out. George has said that sex isn't really terribly important (though he sometimes admits he enjoys it) and, if this is true, then Le Bon is behaving very oddly whenever he gets up on stage, or at any rate overdoing the hip jerking.

Unlike many pop singers, George has become nicer with success. Although now very wealthy, he does not flaunt his wealth. Rather the opposite in fact; George was furious when one of the band went so far as to rent a Porsche. In fact, George says that money is very nice to have but not really all that important, and it isn't hard to believe that he really means this.

George doesn't actually look like getting any poorer! He has started writing songs for other people, and this pursuit can prove very lucrative. So far he has written songs for Musical Youth, Joe Cocker and Petula Clark (she and George are great mutual admirers).

Meanwhile, the public persona goes from strength to strength. Boy George hasn't just made all the magazine covers you'd expect, such as *New Musical Express*, *Melody Maker*, *Record Mirror*, *Smash Hits* and *The Face*, but he also recently made the cover of *Rolling Stone*, *Mad* (as 'Our Boy Neuman'), *Punch*, *TV Times* and even the restrained and highbrow BBC weekly, *The Listener*. There aren't many more places to go. *Time* and *Vogue* perhaps? He's been photographed by Snowdon and caricatured by Giles.

Before he went to Egypt for the first time, he had never been out of England. Now international touring has made the world a familiar place to him, and catching a plane is like catching a London bus! George, and all the members of Culture Club, have coped with their rocket trip to success incredibly well – the g-pull would have been enough to flatten most ordinary mortals. Now they are reaping the rewards and have all bought themselves opulent and well-hidden homes, though it is an open secret that George's is somewhere in London's Little Venice district, one of the richest and most sought-after parts of town.

Whatever happens, George is careful about money. He knows that success at its present rate cannot go on for ever and that it is all too easy to spend, spend, spend – on clothes, instruments and all kinds of other things; so two accountants oversee the ebb and flow of the band's money and two lawyers check out all their contracts and are quick to strike at ripoff merchants, bandwagoners and copycats. They are looking after a valuable commodity: Boy George dolls have overtaken ET dolls in worldwide popularity, and only Michael Jackson stands on an equally high mountain top.

Bifocal

*Sometimes up out of this land
a legend begins to move.
Is it a coming near
of something under love?*

*Love is of the earth only,
the surface, a map of roads
leading wherever go miles
or little bushes nod.*

*Not a legend under,
fixed, inexorable,
deep as the darkest mine
the thick rocks won't tell.*

*As fire burns the leaf
and out of the green appears
the vein in the centre line
and the legend veins under there,*

*So, the world happens twice –
once what we see it as;
second it legends itself
deep, the way it is.*

William Stafford

VII

IMITATORS

'I am a show-off, and that's that. That's how I see myself, and that's how I like to be seen. But it's not all down to the clothes I wear.'

George would not claim that his look is 100 per cent original. He has admitted that he owes a great debt to Philip Sallon, his oldest friend. When he first bumped into Sallon at Bangs club, George encountered an apparition with pit boots, pencil skirt, paper collar and leather gloves. It left a lasting impression: 'He was the first person I saw who really looked original. He was brilliant. Nobody looked like that then.' So George was inspired by Philip Sallon and in turn he has spawned a host of imitators, many of whom have made money in the wake of his success.

One such is Peter Robinson. He was born in Jamaica on 3rd November 1962 but didn't bump into George until much later, around the time when he changed his name to Marilyn after the film star whom he most liked to dress up as. Marilyn claims that he started dressing up and wearing make-up before George, but the leader of Culture Club disputes this, saying that Peter Robinson was 'a very ordinary little soulboy' when he first turned up at one of George's squats. Their friendship, now on/now off, has been a source of delight for the press and a source of publicity for both of them, particularly Marilyn. The low point of this came after a trip they made to Egypt together. At the time George wanted to help Marilyn (who was being groomed for stardom by Haysi Fantayzee manager Paul Caplan) generate a little publicity for himself, but it seems that he took more of the limelight than he was welcome to and they fell out. When Marilyn then sent photographs of an unmade-up Boy George to the national papers, their falling out was considerably more rancorous. In July 1984, however, Marilyn convinced George that there was no point in being enemies, and they spent a two-week holiday together in Jamaica.

Boy George and Marilyn are both effeminate in clothes and style and they have both had records in the charts. But Marilyn, while claiming to be predominantly heterosexual (who cares?), has a great penchant for wearing women's clothes and dressing like Marilyn Monroe, while George's taste is far more equivocal. Though he doesn't wear women's clothes, he doesn't exactly wear men's clothes either.

Marilyn has adopted a female persona and revelled in it. He doesn't have George's philosophy of life, though what he does say often sounds suspiciously like an echo of George. George has firm views on this, saying that if you are going to confront the world with your extravagance and your eccentricity, then you've got to have a serious explanation for why you are doing it.

Pop stars aside, a vast number of fans have taken to copying George's look. The *Sun* newspaper ran a competition for lookalikes in January 1984, and the winner, a 16-year-old from Brighton called Darren Hogg, turned out

to be astonishingly like Boy George. Darren himself has ambitions in the direction of the pop charts, and says with a smile of triumphant recollection that he has been mistakenly mobbed by Culture Club fans. In his role as Doppelganger, he has even appeared on TV-am, one of Britain's breakfast TV channels. But if Darren wants to shine in pop music, he'd better develop an image of his own. There couldn't be more than one Boy George.

Some of the boys who copy George in the way they dress say that it makes them much more attractive to women, and this bears out our hero's accounts of his early experiences. Because you don't seem threatening to them sexually, girls can be more relaxed with you. 'Women definitely think this look is sexy. They don't feel they have to play a role if a man is wearing make-up the way they have to when confronted with a macho-type man. It definitely turns on the girls', reveals one imitator. At the same time the look can suit both sexes and there are plenty of girls out there copying.

Then there are the Gender Benders. These men have not copied George's look in exact details, but rather they have taken his lead in using make-up and glamour to make themselves look more attractive, and more feminine. Unlike him, they tend to wear women's clothes, but this does not necessarily confirm them as transvestites, since their prime motive for doing so is fashion and the fun of dressing up to shock and surprise. They too seem to find that it makes them attractive to girls. The things they say have a familiar ring: 'I simply like to look different and have a horror of looking like everyone else.'

George may have shown the way, but it's not as easy as some people think to express individuality. As George has said, you can't just do it by putting on some make-up and a dress. If that is all you do, you are still a clone. True individuality comes from within and takes courage and hard work. If Boy George changed his image in a radical way – took off that make-up, had his hairdresser give him a crew cut, and put on a grey suit with a blue tie – he'd still be Boy George and actually would probably have little difficulty in carrying off the whole outfit. You can't help feeling that a lot of gender benders would vanish without trace. Not that it matters. The passing show is fun, too. But let's not forget that George was the pioneer; anyone who takes it up after it's been established is just a follower.

Up-and-coming imitators include Robert Girl of The Mystery Girls; DJ-turned-singer Tasty Tim and – in a much less obvious way – Paul, lead singer of King. Tasty Tim says it takes him at least two hours to put his make-up on (and be careful: he found that the glitter he was applying to his lips was made of ground glass) and reckons that everyone should wear make-up. He even claims to have revived the beauty spot.

Imitation, all this, or parallel evolution? And does it matter? The main thing is to be true to yourself. And George always has been.

'My attitude is, that whatever you do, never apologize and never try to defend yourself.'

VIII

THE LOOK

*'Everyone says that I will grow out of this some day,
that I will look back in ten years from now and think
how stupid I looked. The truth is the opposite.'*

At the top of the pop world, you have to run fast to keep up, and George is constantly adjusting his look – tinkering with it, refining it in subtle ways with the result that his appearance is undergoing constant evolution. Compare photos of the past with those of, say, early August 1984, when the sudden blond locks arrived.

There was no look he wouldn't try, from punk to rockabilly to 'cheap Antony Price'. The New Romantic look led naturally to the development of the one that he has made his own, and whose originality defies competition. On the way, he's made imaginative excursions into ancient Rome and the Turkish harem for inspiration. Every costume and every dab of make-up was his own self-taught work. His face became a blank canvas for his self-expression (his battered make-up case even looks a bit like an artist's palette), and that canvas was later to be complemented by his lyrics and Culture Club's music. Although we're talking about his style here, don't forget that it goes hand in hand with his singing nowadays. And it always has done with his personality. 'I think the main thing is my character. I don't think it's my look because most people think I'm going to be a prize prannet who doesn't say anything', he told *New Musical Express* as early as April 1983. 'The Japanese interviewers always say to me, Gosh you're really loud. They analyse me as a sort of quiet David Sylvian character and I'm not like that at all.'

The history of George and his use of make-up acts as a reflection of George's own history and development. In the early days, he used make-up in a stark and strident way but he was always conscious of the way he could disguise the shortcomings of his face. He used to start his preparations with a heavy white foundation and perhaps shade the jawline with a dark brown stick for emphasis. Depending on the effect he wanted he either highlighted his cheeks with blusher, or made his cheekbones more prominent by shading their outline in a dark, dramatic colour – scarlet, brown or black. This line could be extended up above the eyes to the temples, hollowing these too and narrowing the forehead. All this may seem unsubtle but it did the trick of drawing attention to himself.

78

To lengthen the nose, and make it look narrower too, he'd adopt the old stage make-up technique of shading the sides. At one time he preferred to keep his eyebrows plucked, to allow for a dramatic upward sweep of painted brows, which emphasised the eye's orbit, and gave him a greater area in which to use eyeshadow. The eyes themselves, being the most important feature, get the most attention. And he can take the eyeliner right along the inside rim, as well as outside the lashes. The lashes are heavily mascara'd to give his eyes an outline that Cleopatra would have envied. No wonder friends remember him taking over three hours to do it all at the squat.

The foundation and shading would be sealed with a translucent powder. Nowadays, George prefers to follow the natural line of his lips, but he has experimented with a severe, formalised lip-line too.

An added refinement was to draw the eyebrow in in more than one colour.

And to use different coloured varnishes on each nail.

Outside his private circles he is almost never seen without make-up, although nowadays he doesn't worry as much as he used to about this. When he had a row with photographers at Heathrow Airport in August 1983, it was mainly to do with the fact that they had caught him with only a dab of make-up on, and he had absolutely no wish to appear like that on the front pages of all the British newspapers. Nowadays he stresses that his make-up isn't a mask he puts on, or needs to hide behind, but a part of himself. Without the make-up, he's not only *not* the real Boy George, he's *not* the real George O'Dowd, either.

One of the problems he has to contend with is shaving. 'The worst thing about being a man is shaving, because if you cut yourself you have to wait half an hour before you can put your make-up on. So what I usually do is shave before I have a bath, then moisturise my skin, and put on a cream foundation and a translucent fine powder. I also put a bit of touch-up stuff under the eyes and on the top lip – anywhere you are likely to sweat a bit.' He will shave again in the evening before putting on the full make-up. Earlier in his career he shaved his wrists too, though he has ceased to do this now. For one thing, shaving your body hair makes it more and more bristly, 'and in ten years you end up looking like a werewolf'; for another, his sexual ambiguity is becoming a lot less important. There is also a certain anxiety not to be identified with the gay scene (or indeed any other scene – he doesn't want to be put in any category), as happened to him in his initial contacts with the media, particularly in the USA and some European countries.

Although he has always been very chary of getting involved with advertising, such is his mastery of make-up that the New York-based cosmetics

company Elizabeth Arden wanted to use his look as part of a campaign to promote eyeshadow. George wasn't actually using their product, but executives at the cosmetics house felt that he was an inspiration to women to be just as glamorous and daring. He shared the publicity hype with Cher, and Michael Jackson's actress girlfriend, Brooke Shields. 'It's the year of the emphatic eye', ran the publicity material. 'Blue eyes, such as The Boy possesses, denote high intellect and intelligence, fervour and sensitivity, and a deep sincerity.' How successful the campaign will be in the States remains to be seen, but it's hardly in doubt that his command of make-up could certainly be a source of inspiration to many women – if they can face taking their cue from a man.

George's other foray into advertising was almost accidental. George usually wears training shoes, a fact not unnoticed by the shoe manufacturers Puma, who wanted him to wear theirs. Finally, half joking, he gave in to their representatives but *only* if they would make him up a pair that he designed. There and then he drew some shoes on a serviette in the restaurant in Germany (where he was touring at the time). He told Puma that he would wear a pair of these trainers if they made them up for him.

The Puma people seemed horrified and he didn't think that he would see them again after they had gone away. They were persistent, however, and made up the shoes – heavy-duty trainers in primary colours with massive crepe soles, size 10 – and George kept to his word. At concerts, he'll perform barefoot – or he'll wear his Puma trainers. His model in Madame Tussaud's has got them on too – in blue. 'Puma' is written in silver on the tongues.

Ever since KARMA CHAMELEON came out in September 1983, Culture Club have been moving away from the Sue Clowes look. Initially, this move involved Jon, Mikey and Roy wearing costumes based on American football gear or baseball outfits, with George in a new hat – a crimson straw topper with a black brim which, instead of having a crown, opens up like a flower. This was complemented by a dark yellow smock when the band appeared on Top of the Pops to play KARMA CHAMELEON on September 22nd – two days after the single arrived at Number One in the charts. The hat has reappeared since then ... together with a wild suit based on the United States flag. There's also an all-black version of this hat.

The original black hat, which George always wore to begin with, was a Christmas present from a friend, who sent it with the message 'This will bring you luck'. It did. George and the hat were quite inseparable (as I show you in this book) and he even took it with him to extremely hot Egypt. The hat was still on his head early in 1984, although George's clothes were now radically different from those he first wore with it. At a recording session in January for

the American television show The Dick Clark Music Awards (Culture Club for once didn't pick up an award) he wore a calf-length lime-green lurex coat over matching trousers and white boots.

Much interest has always centred on George's hair. For the last three years he has had it looked after by Tina at Antenna, the Kensington hairdressers. The plaits which tumbled from beneath his hat were originally his own, but took longer to organise than any other part of his toilette. So these plaits were replaced by false ones, made of a mixture of real hair and an acrylic called monofibre, which in George's case consisted of a variety of shades based round his natural hair colour, and braided and heatsealed on to George's real hair by a process known as hair extension.

This is a technique that Tina still uses on George's 'new look' hair, and one which Roy Hay, who is also a client, has had done too. The treatment can last a year, but George and Roy have it done relatively frequently, as they take great care of their hair. At a return sitting, the 'extension' hair is taken out and replaced. It's not quite as long a process as it sounds, because the hair extension is joined to the head hair not one by one, but in little bunches. Nevertheless, the whole operation takes about two hours, and in George's case, the hair then has to be curled, which takes another hour. George's hair was blond in August 1984, but when you read this it could be *any* other colour, since he wears it in so many different ways. Plaits make an occasional reappearance, but more often his hair is worn loose, sometimes topped with a bow. Great lengths of hair have come and gone since the orange trowel cut of ten years ago, and from the mad hairdo of his Birmingham days: 'My hair went completely flat, like a plate, on top. I backcombed it, put a hairband round it, and then cut the top like a lawn. I looked like a pink palm tree.'

Jewellery, which was largely missing in the early days of the black hat, is very much in evidence today. And George being George, it's got to be as big and bright and beautiful as possible; you couldn't accuse him of going for subtlety in this department.

George favours heavy diamanté necklaces and pendant earrings. And he seems to share his taste in jewellery with another famous person: British Prime Minister Margaret Thatcher so admired a piece of jewellery made by the young designer Monty Don that he re-created it for her as a 'thank you' present for a reception she'd given for British designers early in 1984. Monty Don is George's favourite designer, and by coincidence he'd already made a very similar piece for him!

'I enjoy dressing up and collecting clothes', says George, and sometimes it seems as if he has even more influence as a Leader Of Fashion than as a singer and songwriter. Although George has said that one day he may

MAKING-UP THE BOY GEORGE WAY

Before applying make-up, clean your face thoroughly and gently apply a good moisturiser. Then, for the best possible result, follow these stages.

1 Dot foundation all over your face, and blend it carefully, either with the tips of your fingers or a damp sponge, extending down your neck and around your ears. If you have shadows under your eyes or any marks or blemishes on your face apply a light-coloured concealer before applying loose, translucent powder onto your face and neck with a big brush.

2 Brush powder blusher on your cheekbones, but no further in than the middle of your eyes.

3 Cover your eyelids with white, pearlised eyeshadow. Outline your socket lines and upper and lower lids with black pencil and then blend the lines with a coloured eyeshadow using a soft brush.

4 Apply highlighter carefully along the brow bone (using a cream highlighter if you have to conceal your eyebrows to make a space for your Boy George eyebrows). With a black kohl pencil draw the eyebrows and a line along the inner rims of the lower lids. Curl your eyelashes with an eyelash curler, then, looking down into a mirror, apply mascara on the top of your top lashes, underneath your top lashes and then mascara your bottom lashes.

5 Outline your lips with a pencil or lip brush, fill in with lipstick and then finish with gloss.

COLOUR YOUR OWN BOY GEORGE

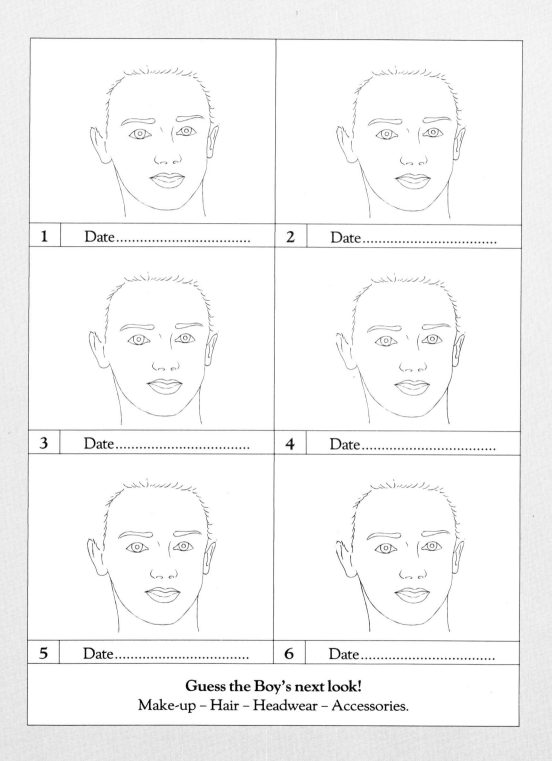

Guess the Boy's next look!
Make-up – Hair – Headwear – Accessories.

retire behind the scenes to concentrate on his writing, it's hard to imagine him being out of the public eye for any length of time. And as indicated by the care he takes over his huge private collection of photographs – which documents stage by stage the development of his image – George has been having a passionate affair with the camera, which would be hard to end.

His new designer is called Dexter Wong and he is a 25-year-old Malaysian with a studio in Marchmont Street and a shop in Hyper Hyper in Kensington. Wong also works with the Thompson Twins. Don't go and ask him to run you up a quick Boy George outfit, though! All the clothes he makes for the singer are strictly one-off and exclusive. Dexter and George have known each other since the days before they were both famous; their long relationship helps each understand what the other wants, and they both work together closely on designs. The first outfit Dexter made for George was the one he wore for the video of CHURCH OF THE POISON MIND. Many more have followed since and, if George likes a basic outfit, he has it made in several colours. And because he wears different clothes on-stage to those he wears in normal life, he has his clothes made up in two different weights: lightweight for concerts – it can get very hot on-stage and also stage clothes need to be light to give plenty of freedom for movement – and thicker material for street wear. The garment design must be versatile enough to look good in either weight, and the one which has been particularly successful has been the long, baggy, belted, smocklike shirt George has been wearing variations of recently.

George designs costumes for himself too, and has recently been working on some for the band's American and British tours in late 1984 and early 1985: these will be very extravagant. During the daytime, and for ordinary street wear, he tends to go for plain colours – often just black or white. His concerts see him take the stage in much brighter ones; for example, the shocking pink outfit that he wears on the cover of COLOUR BY NUMBERS (another Dexter creation), and the bridal getup he wore on THE KISS ACROSS THE OCEAN summer 1984 tour of Japan and Australia. There doesn't seem to be any colour George won't try and he can always adapt his make-up to suit it.

'Whatever you do, do it with style, and it can never be tasteless.'

THE LOOK

Just like the old showbiz cliché, Dexter sometimes sits up all night sewing sequins on to a costume, so that it will be ready for the next day's concert (George himself isn't above doing this), and the two of them continue to plan out ideas together. George's interest in fashion design is growing and 1984 has seen a strong development of his style.

The new look that has been developed for the new album WAKING UP WITH THE HOUSE ON FIRE is called Common Currency and embodies a more colourful, gipsyish attitude, with even a couple of references to punk thrown in. Although Jon, Mikey and Ron are becoming increasingly dressy themselves these days, Culture Club want to get away from their image as superstars and concentrate for a while on music.

Whatever the changes, it seems pretty likely that Culture Club will never be mistaken for any other band, nor for any of their numerous clones. They always manage to keep several steps ahead of the field.

IX

TALK ABOUT THE BOY

*'People think I'm going to be some sort of idiot pouf who's
going to be completely gormless.'*

It's hardly surprising that in two years at the top a band such as Culture Club, and a boy such as George, have attracted a fantastic amount of attention and comment. Many reactions have been hostile, many adoring; some pass the band off as inconsequential, others are merely bewildered. Whether they love them or loathe them, most people have heard of Culture Club.

Early on in his career, George was visiting the Pied Bull, a pub in Islington, North London, which held a gay disco on Saturday nights. George, who says he only wanted a quiet drink and who was quite used to being accepted into the gay community, objected to a notice refusing entry to non-gays – and his quiet drink suddenly got noisy. One of the customers at the bar accused George of betraying the public image of gays, and it was not the first time such a charge had been levelled at him either. 'He said he'd been beaten up for wearing a Gay Pride badge, so I said I'd been in trouble for wearing a Mother's Pride [a brand of sliced bread] badge – he didn't like that.' Meanwhile a gang of skinheads in the neighbouring bar started smashing up the furniture and, when the fun started spilling over into the disco, George did what came naturally to him in the circumstances – he disappeared. Discretion is the better part of valour, as anyone sensible knows. George is actually well able to look after himself in a fight, but which band needs a singer with a broken nose? Not Culture Club anyway.

Several months later there was a fracas at a New Year's Eve party in Ilfracombe, Devon, in the West of England. It had nothing to do with George, who was hundreds of miles away at the time. A mugger dressed as Boy George robbed a woman of a £700 bracelet and necklace, then took off into the night. As it was New Year's Eve, lots of people were in fancy dress and not a few had chosen to go out dressed as Guess Who ... anyway the criminal got away and police said rather desperately afterwards, 'We are appealing to everyone dressed like Boy George to come forward and be eliminated from our enquiries.'

At the beginning of February 1984, an interesting showbusiness encounter took place at the TV Times Awards ceremony in London. Fate brought tough-guy screen actor Robert Mitchum, as straight and as macho as they come, face to face with Boy George. On the whole, they seemed to get on well, though since they are both seasoned professionals in their public behaviour one never quite knows. Afterwards, Mitchum seemed to view the event in an amused light. 'I asked if he was up for adoption. He dresses a bit like a faggot ... but I'm going to adopt him.'

Probably, though, the best-known story about the early part of 1984 was George's famous arrival in France, when he was involved in a fracas with overzealous immigration officials. Two days after the meeting with Mitchum, George left Heathrow Airport on his way to a pop festival in San Remo, Italy.

MAD ABOUT THE BOY

He was travelling via Nice, and took a Japanese dancer friend called Mitsuko with him. That in itself – and the fact that they held hands – was enough to start press tongues wagging and telex wires buzzing, but she was dressed as a geisha, and he wore a stunning red and blue kimono dotted with Culture Club symbols. Much later George admitted that they'd worn the costumes as a lead into the video for IT'S A MIRACLE, which is intended to have a Japanese feel. As they left England, George firmly discouraged any romantic linking of his name with Mitsuko's. So far it had been a quiet trip!

France is a conservative country in many ways, and the French tend to be more reserved than other Europeans. George disembarked at Nice Airport and approached passport control. He handed in his passport.

The officer looked at it, looked at George, and shook his head. At this point George, who had travelled to America, Canada, Germany, Austria, Spain, Italy, Japan and Hong Kong on tours without any bother before, was not expecting trouble. The immigration man took him to an office. He pointed out that the passport showed the photograph of a young man. What was giving him cause for doubt, he explained, was that he saw a young woman in front of him. George was therefore refused entry to France – unless of course he would care to prove that he was the person in the passport photograph by taking off his make-up, or by any other means.

George does not suffer fools gladly, and his temper can operate on a short fuse. He hit the roof, but the French official still refused to give way. The argument went on for three hours. Outside, French fans waited impatiently, while George and manager Tony Gordon tried to make the officials change

" DIDN'T I WARN YOU TO KEEP AWAY FROM BOY GEORGE!"

their minds. They wouldn't, and nor would George. The British Consulate in Nice was contacted. The French officials were informed that George was an international artist and that the way he looked was an integral part of his art.

Finally, the French gave way, ruefully explaining that they had after all been bound by immigration rules that don't allow the admission of transvestites and it would have been more than their job was worth to admit George. Obviously, this was an error in thinking; George is not a transvestite. But George had the last laugh. 'They stopped our lamb but they couldn't stop me' said our triumphant hero, rapidly recovering his aplomb and referring to a Common Market argument over imported meat.

There was more fuss on arrival at San Remo. The romantic link between Mitsuko and George had to be scotched again, as did impudent direct questions about his homosexuality. When Mitsuko left for London there was a tearful farewell, but she told the press, 'We are just good friends.' And George, ever astute in handling the journalists who dog his every footstep, pointed out: 'I think it would be wrong if I were to appear in public having a close physical relationship, with either a man or a woman. That would anger my fans.'

But on his return to England, rumours of a romance still had to be stamped out. A photo of George and Mitsuko kissing had appeared in the papers. 'I kiss everybody', retorted George, and promptly kissed thirty of the fans who were waiting at the airport to welcome him back. One of them, left breathless, said he was a wonderful kisser – but he left a lipstick mark on *her* lips!

In America, Culture Club first made their mark as musicians. People had heard their records but had no idea of what they looked like ... and more specifically what George looked like. They got a shock when they finally found out. Some people described him as a walking disaster, and a Detroit DJ by name of Dick Purton actually organised a protest; he suggested that fans go to the concert in Detroit and hear the music they liked, but in order to avoid George's siren looks they should all wear blindfolds! The protest, started for fun, attracted 3000 protesters but they were laughed out of court by other fans when they got to the concert, and encountered the Boy George magic.

Even the narrowest mind finds it hard to resist George's charm, and disapproval always seems to rebound on the disapprover; George is able to get people to look beyond the clothes and the make-up, to *him*. And when they do, they encounter affection rather than the conceit usual in many pop stars! This may be the reason why he is so universally accepted. His clothes and appearance gain him attention and then he wins people over through his charm and humour and intelligence. With Boy George, the average fan is not buying 'sexual ambiguity' (this really doesn't matter), so much as accepting a talented singer who sings songs which touch on everyone's problems and preoccupations in a very straightforward and intelligent way.

George's style was pretty hard for his family to accept, but finally they came to terms with it and are now very proud. Success always helps. 'I was a rifleman in the army,' said his father, 'and I just couldn't understand the idea of a boy of mine wearing make-up ... but really there is room for all kinds of people in this world. Everybody should be free to do whatever it is that makes them happy, so long as it doesn't hurt anyone else.'

His mum remembers that 'when I first saw him like this, I thought, Oh, no. But it's like everything else with him – he's got a valid argument for it. Like most parents, I used to worry about what the neighbours were going to think. But George taught me not to be concerned about that, and now I don't care.' And she has seen how dedicated George is to his fans: 'George works ever so hard – especially at keeping in touch with his fans. Do you know he sat down at the kitchen table all afternoon and signed 2000 photos for people who had written in.'

His father remembers George at work: 'He'll sit at the kitchen table and knock out a song or two. Then he'll say, "What do you think of that, Mum?", or "How about this one, Dad?" ' His mother thinks 'the music's wonderful and the words are interesting too.' His younger brother Gerald says, 'I'm a labourer and the blokes on the site think he's great. Even those who say he's a pouf still like him. I think he's clever and witty.'

Jon Moss says of him, 'Everybody really likes him; he's very lovable', and Mikey recalls their first meeting: 'I sensed a lot of power round him, and strength. I liked that.'

But you can't please all of the people all the time, and not everybody has been complimentary. A security man who saw him off (George was in minimal make-up at the time) to New York on Concorde drily remarked, 'He looked as if he needed a good trip through a sheep dip', though this was in the wake of the row with the photographers. That that incident is remembered proves just how rare it is for George to let the charming public image slip. He hints that sometimes he behaves deliberately badly because every so often 'you've got to show a little of the mean side of yourself.' His ability to turn even the worst situations to his advantage is borne out by the comments of his press aide, who says, 'George isn't simply someone who gets up there and sings and leaves it at that. He's very shrewd – in many ways a self-manager. He takes an interest in every single aspect of the group, the music, promotion, earnings, investment – everything.'

Prince of drag Danny La Rue says, 'I think he is very clever. I like

Remember the Rose

Words by Sidney D. Mitchell

Music by Seymour B. Simons

Sung by

BERT ERROL

Copyright. Price 2/- nett cash

B. FELDMAN & Co.
125, 127, 129, Shaftesbury Avenue, W.C.2.
LONDON, ENGLAND.

ROLAND'S PIANOFORTE TUTOR THE BEST IN THE WORLD.
English and Foreign Fingering.

New York & Detroit: JEROME H. REMICK & Co. Copyright in U.S.A. by Jerome H. Remick & Co.

TALK ABOUT THE BOY

anything that works. Gimmicks are fine if you have the talent to back it up. George has the talent. A frock and a wig are not enough. You have to have a mind – and that's how you make things work.'

Another facet of the Boy's character is illustrated by a comment from Helen Terry, the band's principal backing singer (who recently launched her own solo career with the active support of Roy and George). 'George has this big woman complex. He's really into the big mother figure. Not that he sees me as a mother figure, he just likes the idea!'

Generally he has attracted a wide range of comments. Neil Sedaka is rather cool about him. 'Boy George is a great personality, but that has never been enough on its own; people soon see through that. But he makes good records. If he didn't you could forget about him immediately. No matter how outrageous he was, it would mean nothing.' Rod Stewart is less restrained: 'He has the most soulful voice I've heard in years', and the former Beatles producer and elder statesman of the pop world, George Martin, says: 'He has a much better voice than half the other singers around, and he definitely has a future.' Before he realised that George was a boy, Ronnie Wood of the Rolling Stones tried to date him, or so said a grinning Keith Richards.

At the end of 1983 George was able to meet two of the stars of his favourite television programme. Elizabeth Dawn, who plays Vera Duckworth in Coronation Street, was completely won over: 'He's gorgeous. My three daughters will be green with envy when I tell them Mum gave him a cuddle'; Tracie Bennet, who plays Sharon, was just as keen: 'He's great ... a really smashing performer.'

Adverse publicity for George came at the beginning of 1984 when Hollywood dress designer 'Mr Blackwell' named Boy George '1983's fourth worst-dressed woman in the world' – not even worst-dressed but fourth worst, how low can anyone sink! Winner of this uncoveted title was Joan Collins, now an occasional neighbour of George in Little Venice. 'Fashionwise, he's enough to give drag a bad name,' intoned 'Mr Blackwell'. 'If he wants to dress up to look like the worst-dressed girl in town, then he can't complain if he ends up on my list.'

George's sense of style has caused some consternation amongst scien–

tists and psychologists too. People-watcher Desmond Morris has this to say: 'The fact is that the wearing of pseudo-female costume reflects the anti-macho campaign. It is trying to get a more balanced, sensible relationship between the sexes ... There is nothing inherently unmasculine about putting on costume and make-up. It is no more effeminate than an African warrior who spends several hours putting on make-up to make himself look fierce.' Dr Vernon Coleman says, 'In the animal kingdom, the male of the species is often far more attractive than the female and does all the strutting and ritual dancing. The whole phenomenon [of boys dressing as girls] ... is a reflection of the pressures on men that have come about from the growing influence of the women's movements. Many men simply don't know what is expected of them any more or what role they are expected to play.'

But listen, men in England *used* to dress up all the time, before the Victorians came along and put a stop to it. An aristocrat of the eighteenth century, with his ornate brocaded jackets and towering wigs, would put George to shame.

'No-one laughs at priests because they wear dresses – their clothes are accepted.'

Psychologist Dr John Nicholson (who's written a book called 'Men and Women – How Different Are They?') admits some of the bewilderment and part of the futility in seeking such an explanation. Some things are unanswerable: 'If you are a woman and you are attracted to Boy George or Marilyn, it is not necessarily because you want to go to bed with them. This age of the gender benders seems to me to be a period of considerable sexual confusion.'

Closer to home, Jon Moss prefers to talk about the singer's personality: 'George knows how to create images and inspire people. He's like a painter, and he paints with clothes and people.' Former girlfriend Tracey Birch says disarmingly, 'It just wouldn't occur to him to make advances.'

Old friends from his squats days have mixed memories of George, but the picture is fairly consistent. 'He may look soft, but in his head he's very tough. When kids in the street started to throw stones at us, he really took them on. At first their parents hated us too, but George soon had them eating out of his hand. They'd invite him round for tea and give him clothes, treat him like the Queen Mother.'

'He would cast affection on only one person at a time, and his devotion was total', Stephen Jones says. 'He is one of the most starlike people that I have ever met. I never doubted that he would be successful ... I realised that he had a wonderful voice. At the time we all said he ought to be making his living by singing. But I don't think that the time was right then, and George was a clever boy, so he waited until it was.'

What about the famous bitchiness? 'It's a kind of Bet Lynch bitchiness – the tart with a heart of gold. He gets wild but he's very humorous too.'

Almost everyone who comes across him has an opinion about Boy George. An elderly security guard at Culture Club's concert at the Memorial Auditorium in Buffalo, upstate New York: 'That guy, well, he's just something else ... I just thought this would be some British faggot screaming out of tune. It wasn't like that. I'm converted.' Consider a reader of the *Daily Mirror* a few days after that newspaper had printed a picture of Australian lady body-builder Bev Lewis. The reader wrote, whether joking or not, 'What a nice girlfriend Bev Lewis would make for Boy George.'

But the last words in this chapter really have to go to Princess Margaret, to whom Boy George was presented in 1984 at a radio awards ceremony at the London Hilton. (She later refused to have her photograph taken standing next to him.) After she'd met him, she turned away and discreetly asked: 'Boy who?'

'I don't believe in marriage. If you love someone you don't have to prove it. The thing is, I can go two ways on that subject, because if you love someone you're going to want to keep them forever aren't you? You can't be dogmatic about love, it's such a heartrending thing. I'm sure I'd get married if I loved someone.'

X

CULTURE CLUB

*'It's multicultural. I'm Jewish, George is Catholic and dresses up,
Mikey is black and Roy is like a typical English boy.' (Jon)*

Behind all the publicity that surrounded Boy George, the band was steadily notching up a series of singles, not one of which failed to make the Top Five. Reviews of DO YOU REALLY WANT TO HURT ME? were mixed. Thomas Dolby (with whom Jon had done a gig when he was with Eskimo Norbert) was enthusiastic, as were Mark Cooper and Danny Baker. Others wrote about 'weak watered down fourth division reggae' and 'an unremarkable whinge with a soft underbelly'. The public had chosen, however, and by the time the first album, KISSING TO BE CLEVER, came out a month later, Culture Club had already begun to find more favour. As we've seen, it was a gamble. Out of their three singles to date, two had fared badly, and DO YOU REALLY WANT TO HURT ME? didn't hit Number One until a week after the album was released. KISSING TO BE CLEVER was hailed as being 'characterised by real application, enthusiasm and self-awareness', and Boy George was seen as a true artist, not as the *poseur* some had suspected him of being. Despite the almost confusing variety of influences the songs displayed, what got people going was their freshness, and their ability to use those influences to form a new, whole entity. They hit the mark by their professionalism and by their 'reaffirmation of life's values in a crumbling world'. At the same time it was recognised that the album had been cleverly packaged and marketed too, so you could say that the whole thing was a calculated miracle.

On the verge of real fame, Boy George remembers going into a hamburger takeaway in Oxford Street. 'I was dressed up and I forgot. I mean, I don't feel there is anything *to* forget. I was hungry and thought I'd better get something to eat. These little kids got round me in a circle, poking me. It was quite amusing, because they kept saying, "Are you the girl from Culture Club?"...' His personal fame has always been in danger of obscuring the other members of the group from the public eye and this is one reason why he takes such pains to point out the unity of the band. He feels that the band should operate in much the same way as a family – an informal but close association based on love; a unit that fights adversity and copes with success together. One for all and all for one. 'I really liked Roy as soon as I met him. He was quiet, he didn't have a big mouth. There are no Flash Harrys in this band.' That comes across in performance, too. There's nothing over the top about George's stage mannerisms. If anything, and it seems like a paradox, there's a gauche graciousness about him. It's not 'pantomime dame' but at a very sophisticated level it *could* be.

George has described the whole collection on KISSING TO BE CLEVER as cynical love songs, and his attitude to people is tempered with cynicism too. Those who used to jeer at him now seek his autograph. But the

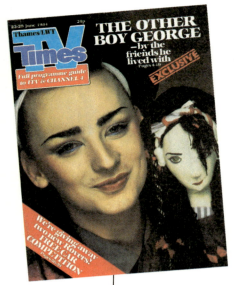

response to the band has been cynical too, at times. Culture Club have been accused of having no soul – of being professionally packaged and competent, but lacking the vital spark. MOR? Radio 2? ABBA-ish? They may have gone on to make the majority change their minds about them, but a few sceptics remain. Nowadays it makes no difference. The effect is what's important. Certainly it had been established that Boy George was not just a pretty face, and that Culture Club was not going to be just another fly-by-night band. The accent was on quality, the inspiration romantic rather than sexual, and the stance political only in the broadest sense. The delivery, always, professional, unaffected and charming. No other group at the moment comes close.

Things moved fast. In February 1983 George was awarded the *Daily Mirror* Readers' Award for Outstanding Musical Personality, and Culture Club took second place (to Duran Duran) in the British Rock and Pop Awards Best Group section. The following year George was again voted the Outstanding Musical Personality, and Culture Club took the award for Best Single with KARMA CHAMELEON. Two months after that, Culture Club were voted Europe's top group at Cannes in a poll conducted through 60 million televison magazine readers in nine European countries. In America, the band picked up a Grammy for Best New Artists. KARMA CHAMELEON was again the record responsible for the award, but already three singles from the album KISSING TO BE CLEVER had got into the US Top Ten, the first time such a thing had happened since The Beatles. When the British Record industry announced their awards, KARMA CHAMELEON topped the best-selling single list for the year and the band also picked up the title Best British Group. All this must have pleased *NME's* Danny Baker, the reviewer who had supported the the band from the first, and who had predicted Number One success for KARMA CHAMELEON – five days after it was released and ten days before it hit the top spot!

KARMA CHAMELEON, with its lilting, carefree beat that owes something to blue grass, and nods in the direction of The Eagles and The Beach Boys, was the second real mountain top, in terms of overall popularity, that Culture Club reached. Like every song, it was different from the ones that had gone before, and yet it has the unmistakable Culture Club seal on it – a lightness of touch and a rolling of rhythm.

CULTURE CLUB

But the group is not standing still, and it's likely that there will be more mountain tops soon. IT'S A MIRACLE was the third single to reach Number One in the UK, in April 1984.

1983 rolled by with tours of the USA, Europe and Japan as well as the UK – the final part of which had to be postponed when Jon cracked his wrist outside Sheffield City Hall, after the tour bus hit a kerbstone. The fans who had bought tickets were not disappointed, however, as Culture Club came back and finished the tour later.

George was becoming larger than life – he seemed to be everywhere. On magazine covers, on TV shows, his voice coming out of transistor radios in all sorts of places or his face on video jukeboxes. He was virtually inescapable. And so he became a media superstar, a personality known to everyone, pursued by advertising agencies, courted by chat show producers, followed by journalists and dogged by photographers. Comedians did take-offs, cartoonists drew caricatures, his name and exploits made it into the editorial columns of national newspapers. He was instantly recognised everywhere.

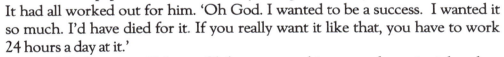

It had all worked out for him. 'Oh God. I wanted to be a success. I wanted it so much. I'd have died for it. If you really want it like that, you have to work 24 hours a day at it.'

All the time Culture Club were working out the principles they believed in. There was no question of threatening violence or threatening anything at all, they wanted to change things from within. 'You put across ideas that hopefully people will take up,' says Jon, 'but you can't force them to do anything. All you can do is present them with things, and put them in a way they will understand ... The keyword with Culture Club is communication. At our gigs they scream, but when we start playing they stop because they want to listen.' He says that George's lyrics hit emotions bang on. You've got to trust the lyrics too. Little girls at the concerts understand their meaning better than Jon does himself.

Some of the songs have been thought better in their depth and feeling than others. BLACK MONEY, TIME (CLOCK OF THE HEART), THAT'S THE WAY and VICTIMS may not have had the success of the most popular songs (though both TIME and VICTIMS reached Number Three) but they may point the way to Culture Club's future development.

Whatever happens though, the band won't compromise. They will do adverts only for specific reasons and have turned down millions of dollars' worth of offers. This year, Culture Club rejected the sum of $300,000 to play

MAD ABOUT THE BOY

'Americans are more involved with the music and less concerned with the image.'

'I don't feel like a superstar. In a lot of ways I'm very humorous – like Liberace and Charlie Chaplin.'

TALK ABOUT THE BOY

'I'm not frightened of not being successful; I'm frightened of not being successful as a person.'

'I always deal with my problems.'

105

at the wedding of a Dallas magnate's daughter's wedding – for half an hour. The money, by this stage, has become only incidental to their work.

One of the things that sets this band apart from most others is the fact that Culture Club are constantly seeking to break down the barriers between them and the audience – they prefer not to cultivate any feeling of 'them and us'. Typically, George now cares less if his make-up runs a little on stage when he gets sweaty. Once he is up there working, he's one of the team, however much he may stand apart from them in the world outside. The music and the audience come first, and if his image gets a little shiny, well, it's strong enough to take it.

Naturally there's been friction within the band, and jealousy of the fact that George has got the lion's share of publicity. Matters weren't helped by George's habit of calling the Club *my band*. But the near-split on the second American tour of 1983 made everybody realise that without each other success would just disappear: Roy and Mikey had to look to Jon for experience of the music world; Roy and Mikey provided stability; Jon and George provided the sparks; Roy provided the patience to build up the music and lay down the tracks – they all contributed to the whole.

With no official leader, ideas have to be sorted out amongst the four of them, and however much it might be George's natural impulse to lead, running the Club is a shared responsibility. Sometimes working from the lyrics of George, at other times from Jon's pre-recorded drum beat, Roy has the task of sorting out the melodic line – but, just as he has some say in what George writes (though George's ultimate control over what he writes is tight, and getting tighter), so the melody will be criticised and then worked out between them all. This process can mean weeks of argument followed by a few days' concentrated work in which the song is actually and finally created. And then you've got to overlay how well they get on as people. George has said that he has less in common with Roy and Mikey than with Jon, and that, whereas he can come to some kind of understanding pretty quickly with Jon, rows can flare up more

" DAMMIT! YOU'RE IMPROPERLY DRESSED AGAIN!"

easily between him and Roy and him and Mikey. He's even said, 'Sometimes I wonder what I'm doing in this band!' After all, they've only known each other for two or three years, and working in a small group of people under constant pressure can put a lot of tension on everybody; though of course their success has to some extent mollified the situation and gives them every incentive to stick together. 'We know that the band is a magical mixture and that if any one member decided to leave, it would collapse', says Jon.

To sum up, George supplies most of the lyrics, Roy many of the harmonies, Mikey conceptualises, and Jon provides the overall shape. No wonder the credit on the album sleeves reads simply, 'Music and lyrics by Culture Club'.

'The good thing is that in this band I have three other people with me, to keep me on the ground. I know I wouldn't be anything without them.'

Just as few people see George beneath the make-up, so there aren't many who have seen his body underneath the flowing robes. Wham! and Duran Duran may flaunt their bodies and flex their muscles for the camera, but George goes his own, original way. It is a policy which keeps people guessing. Everyone knows what most groups look like in a fairly detailed way but what is George like underneath the robes? With George you hardly even get a glimpse of forearm.

One of Boy George's favourite singles is Blue Mink's MELTING POT, which Culture Club do a version of. If everyone could be put in a great big melting pot, so the words of the song go, everybody would come out all mixed up and the differences between people and races would disappear. George really believes in a multicultural and multiracial world, and he aims to put the message across in the most soulful way possible. Up until her recent departure, the band have had added support on the soul front from their principal back-up singer, Helen Terry, a plump 27-year-old white lady from Essex. And what a voice she has ... Michael Jackson has called her the best soul singer since Aretha Franklin. Helen figures prominently on the COLOUR BY NUMBERS album and virtually became the fifth member of the group, but her talent was noticed by various people in the record industry and she could not resist the opportunity to embark on a solo career.

Helen released her debut single LOVE LIES LOST on 30th April 1984, just over a year after she first joined Culture Club, and is now signed to a six-year contract with Virgin Records worth at least £100,000 a year. Her

debut album appeared in the autumn of 1984. LOVE LIES LOST was written by Helen, with someone called Roy Hay and another member of his band by name of G. O'Dowd. Percussion was by Jon Moss, and the single enjoyed reasonable success in the UK. George and Roy were also heavily involved in creating the album – and the producer was the man who produces for Culture Club, Steve Levine. With all that help behind her and that voice, too, Helen looks set fair for a fantastic career. Culture Club will miss her, but they also wish her the very best of luck. Other regulars who play with the band are trumpeter Terry Bailey (ex-Teardrop Explodes), former Sailor keyboardist Phil Pickett and sax player Steve Grainger.

Their success abroad makes them a valuable invisible export, and while the government may not be doling out the CBEs yet (The Beatles are still the only group to hold that honour), there's been a good deal of talk in government circles about tabling a motion to congratulate Culture Club and other leading bands on what they've done. After the doldrums of the Seventies, British record companies now hold an amazing 35 per cent of the vitally important US market, and that's thanks to groups like Culture Club, Duran Duran, and The Police, and their success Stateside. There's now a new sense of confidence in British pop. The idea of official congratulation finds a lot of favour with Jon: 'I think they're pleased that something good has come out of Britain. I think it's great. I'm really pleased about it.' What's amazing is that all this has happened in two short years. Is it that they've successfully 'plagiarised' and then brilliantly repackaged an array of musical types in a way that makes for 'nice and easy' listening? Or is it *more* than that? Is it that their synthesis of sound really makes for a new music, with its own identity, but a music which every culture and every age group can respond to? Jon says, 'I think the hardest thing in the world is to write a good pop song. If you ask me, it's much easier to write music that appeals to a small group of people. Yet we're not in a typical pop band. You can't categorise us. We don't follow any one musical line. Every single we've released has been different.' Jon sees his task as keeping the band as a band. 'I'm trying to make everybody remember it's a job, and we have a responsibility to people. We have a drink now and then, but we don't do drugs ... We're here to work. We're not The Osmonds, but a guy who runs First National Bank doesn't go around smashing up his house and getting pissed every night just because he's rich and successful. So why should a band do it? If you respect and love what you do, then you should make bloody sure you keep on doing it.'

And to think that David Croft of the BBC turned them down in the early days when they approached him to play on RIVERSIDE. Still, we all make mistakes.

XI

THE FANS

*'I'm sure the girls weren't intending to tear us limb from limb –
at least, I hope not!'*

Boy George has lots of time for Culture Club fans. He doesn't consider their presence to be an invasion of his privacy, either, and finds it easy to talk to them in a perfectly natural way, because after the initial excitement of meeting him disappears and they find their tongues again, they usually discover that they have plenty in common with him, and he with them in turn. He still reads the music press and still goes out and buys records. He's not a millionaire recluse living in some ivory tower.

Somewhat cruelly, the band's followers have been nicknamed 'Culture Vultures', since they hover around the boys waiting for any scraps that may come their way. Most of the fans are girls and many favour dressing like George – though they find it hard to keep up with his shifts in image. They shower him with gifts – teddy bears and dolls mainly; George reckons he has about 8000 dolls in his collection.

The attraction is strong. Four girls from the North of England have followed the band religiously on their tours, seeing them night after night in place after place. They've Greyhound-bussed it in America, hitched throughout Europe and slept anywhere they could. It's a story of incredible dedication; these girls have spent all their spare time and money trailing their heroes from place to place to place.

Culture Club do, however, keep fans at a sensible distance and never encourage groupies. They've learnt the lesson of those bands who have gone before them and who have had fights on the road, destroyed themselves with any number of excesses and generally messed up their lives and music through indulgence. 'In this business it's very difficult to have a relationship. Groupies aren't worth it. It's futile. It's fantasy. It's not as if they want you because they think you're wonderful. In the morning you look like an ugly bastard with a big nose and spots just like anyone else. They want you because you've got money and you are a pop star . . . What they are offering is not real. It's not yours. The way they're giving it to you is just a sick thing. When you make love to someone it has got to be passionate – not as if you're making love to a brick.'

It isn't easy to pin down Culture Club fans. They fall into many categories. The Club don't command an exclusively teenage girl audience such as Wham! or Duran Duran do. They seem to cover just about everybody;

there are even a few grandpas out there who like them and there are plenty of grandmas 'I've had really beautiful poems from grannies', says George, and his idea of how the band puts itself across goes a long way towards explaining how quickly people have been won over to the Culture cause after those initial reactions of shock at George's appearance. 'I hate those old-fashioned rock and roll artists. They sleep with their fans, they take cocaine, they drink too much. And they spend their whole time allowing their success to become an extension of their personalities. I think that that's the worst thing that can happen to you. The whole idea of rock and roll having to be sexy and risqué and threatening is so old-fashioned . . . I don't believe in the generation gap. It's harmful rubbish. The alienation of pop from older people is lessening now. That's good.' The message of Culture Club is for everyone. There are no barriers.

Turning his power to good, a twenty-minute taped message from Boy George was enough to bring one child out of an apparently permanent coma; and a 19-year-old anorexic fan from Essex was cured just by example. She'd been to a Culture Club concert, loved it and joined the fan club. Thinking about what George says, she realised that personality is much more important than looks. Now she's eating again, is up from five to eight stone, and all she wants to do is meet Boy George and thank him personally.

Adoration can create problems though. One American fan, a 23-year-old from Buffalo, was so obsessed by George that it put her marriage on the rocks. The reason for this was that she dressed like George all the time, never stopped talking about him, and even got up in the middle of the night to play his records. Can you blame her husband for getting annoyed? When told of this, George gave her a message: 'I don't think you should risk your marriage for me . . . I want to know that everyone is happy and no one, boy or girl, should get their knickers in a twist over me. I'm just a singer, a musician, and people should judge me on our music alone. OK?' But what do you do

THE FANS

'Love is the most important thing in the world.
Everyone wants to be needed, and everyone wants
to be loved.'

THE FANS

when parents turn up to your concerts with their 3-year-old children dressed up like you?

The Boy George look has gone international. Clothes shops everywhere fill their windows with George-inspired clothing and boys from the Philippines to Finland are nicking their girlfriends' make-up. His reputation has gone as far as Russia, though a recent attempt to organise a Culture Club tour there came to nothing. It seems that the Soviets thought their youth might be corrupted.

The Principal Reason for all this says modestly, 'I'm very average looking, but I think I make the best of myself. I believe I can transform myself with make-up.' At the end of 1983, George was attributing his success to working-class appeal. 'The Princess of Wales certainly doesn't buy my records.' Events proved him wrong a short time afterwards, when early in 1984 Culture Club were invited to do a concert before the Prince and Princess of Wales and one of the charities they support. Diana is a keen pop fan. However, Culture Club couldn't meet the time appointed for the performance, and regretfully had to pull out of their date with Royalty.

117

XII

PASS IT ON AFRICA

*'I'm trying to open people's minds and make them more
tolerant of things which aren't harmful.'*

The end of August 1984 saw the release of a new film from Virgin, co-distributed with 20th Century Fox. Called 'Electric Dreams', it was directed by Steve Barron from a story by Rusty Lemorande. The film is a romantic tragi-comedy about a home computer called Edgar, which falls in love with its owner's girlfriend. Original music from the film is by (among others) Giorgio Moroder, Jeff Lynn, Helen Terry, Heaven 17 and Culture Club.

The band have two songs in the film. The first, LOVE IS LOVE, is supposedly composed by Edgar at his owner's request to serenade the girl in question – shades of Cyrano de Bergerac! LOVE IS LOVE is the first conventional love song George has written and it is the vehicle for the most sustained lyrics and most fully realised music yet produced by Culture Club. The second song, which is heard shortly afterwards, is called THE DREAM and accompanies a passage in the film where the computer is dreaming. This song too is an advance and demonstrates just how far Culture Club have come, as well as how far they are capable of going in the future. The orchestration of both songs is superb, making the fullest use of modern electronic recording effects, while losing none of their lyrics' emotional power. While THE DREAM may be faintly reminiscent of IT'S A MIRACLE (Culture Club's third Number One), LOVE IS LOVE is all new and belongs less to the world of pop than to the realms of cabaret and film; George is determined to experiment. (DO YOU REALLY WANT TO HURT ME? and KARMA CHAMELEON are both in the soundtrack of the film, too, but as instrumental versions.) A third new song, HELLO GOODBYE, originally intended for 'Electric Dreams' too, was released as a single in summer 1984. It represents another new departure for the band: a cross somewhere between Led Zeppelin and James Brown. On the flip side is a rock and roll number called CRIME TIME. Sometimes you have to pinch yourself to remember just how short a time it has taken them to produce so much great music.

Autumn 1984 also saw the third album. Called WAKING UP WITH THE HOUSE ON FIRE, it contains a new element; it is a much tougher, harder beat and this gives the album a feel quite distinct from the previous two. All the tracks are new and none of them will be issued later as 'B' sides on singles. Since WAKING UP WITH THE HOUSE ON FIRE comes about a year after the release of COLOUR BY NUMBERS, we have further proof that the band is showing no signs of slowing up, or letting imagination run out on them.

Some songs reflect earlier and continuing themes, like CLONE WAR, which deals with the need to maintain individuality; and the ideas in BLACK MONEY, about the effect of money and success on a person, are followed

through as well. There's a song about superstardom and identity, and another autobiographical one, this time about George's schooldays and childhood. This is called UNFORTUNATE THING.

After the ups and downs of 1983 and the frenetic energy expended on travel, coupled with the tension of coming to terms with success, Culture Club have had a year in which to consolidate the gains of the previous one ... and the four of them are now gelling happily as well as successfully. Mikey has retained that gorgeous grin, though he's started taking the work more seriously. Roy's gaining confidence and this is revealed in the way he has now developed a look of his own – the blond hair is worn long down his back and over the shoulders, he puts on green eyeshadow and is much more adventurous in how he dresses, with current favourite outfits now including a blue lurex suit and a white kaftan with a broad black belt. Jon is moving more and more into production; and he's learning the piano again, and beginning to write lyrics. He mixed the live video of the Christmas concert at the Hammersmith Odeon, A KISS ACROSS THE OCEAN.

The images the band are now using are bolder and more varied – the Sue Clowes symbols and the Japanese characters, as I have said, are giving way to numbers written large in black or primary colours on white; pound and dollar signs; an oriental dancing girl taken from an old print; costumes based on the Union Jack but spangled in diamanté. (See the IT'S A MIRACLE video, which is in part a celebration of being British.)

George's clothes, perhaps reflecting success, are becoming richer in texture and colour. Deep reds, oranges and yellows worn usually with black. Those distinctive Puma trainers in red or blue with white flashes, soles and laces. More formal blue and silver lurex lined in soft white silk. A silver straw hat has made several appearances, and so have long, shiny black gloves.

But the most dramatic development in Boy George's appearance is in the hair and face. Worn naturally long, his hair has a carefully tousled look which makes him look as if he has spent a lot less time preparing to go out: he wears this equally effectively up, straight down, or combed to one side of the head. When he returned from Jamaica with Marilyn in July 1984, his hair was quite blond and worn long still in a frothy curly style. Since he seldom wears a hat now, one's attention is focused more on his face, where the make-up is altogether softer and more subtle. Although he sometimes employs a make-up artist now, his ability to do it himself surpasses many professionals, as viewers of 'The Tube' in July 1984 in Britain witnessed.

George's eyes are still rimmed heavily in black and the lipstick hugs the natural curve of his lips, but in dramatic red against very pale foundation. Instead of being framed by dark plaits, his face is now (usually) framed by

PASS IT ON AFRICA

ringlets or very heavy pendant earrings. The effect greatly increases the femininity of George's face and enhances the impression created by the new clothes – but the whole is an extension of all that existed before rather than a departure from it. Having said that, the new look is also a push further into territory where many clones may dare not follow. George's parents were able to join him for the Australian leg of the Club's summer tour, after which George took himself off to Jamaica for a fortnight's holiday. But there was another surprise in store for fans and pressmen alike: George, typically unpredictable, had his hair dyed blond, and not only cut his make-up down to an absolute minimum but started a modest growth of beard as well !

After their brief summer break, the band settled down to putting the finishing touches to WAKING UP WITH THE HOUSE ON FIRE. The new album – the first to be in a gatefold sleeve – looks to Africa for some of its inspiration, and the African theme is reflected in the LP's cover. Helen Terry and Adele Harris supply backing vocals, and Roy has introduced two new machines to his musical line-up: a DXI synthesiser and a guitar synthesiser. He's especially happy with the guitar synth!

As if all this were not enough, George is also working on a song with Pat Arnold (the Sixties singer best remembered for THE FIRST CUT IS THE DEEPEST), who also sang the title song from 'Electric Dreams'. And Mikey is settling into a luxurious new flat, where he lives along with a bewildering array of machinery (from dishwashers to microwaves). After the Japan/Australia tour he took a ballooning holiday in Africa and when he got back he moved in.

Mikey learnt to water-ski very well towards the end of the spring tour in the USA – on alligator-infested waters – and wants to do some more. On that tour, he remembers how at one gig their dresser, Bill, left a coat-hanger in George's costume after a quick change during CHURCH OF THE POISON MIND. Members of the Club wondered if next day they'd see lots of fans wandering round town with coat-hangers sticking out from their collars – following Boy George's latest fashion lead!

Other things haven't changed at all. Being the most original, attractive and professional band around doesn't just happen – you have to work at it. There are the business affairs of the organization to be attended to, and, above all, the words and the music to be created, worked at, and refined.

In the end it's the songs that matter most.

THE BOY GEORGE AND CULTURE CLUB QUIZ

1 What is Boy George's full real name?
2 Which was Culture Club's first record to go to Number One in the UK charts?
3 Who was the last member of the band to join it?
4 Which of the four members of the band does not come from London?
5 What is the name of the oldest member of the band?
6 What is the exact date of birth of the oldest member of the band?
7 Where was Boy George born?
8 Which two members of Culture Club grew up south of the River Thames?
9 Which was the second Culture Club single to reach Number One in the UK charts?
10 How did the COLOUR BY NUMBERS album score an all-time 'first' for a band in Canada?
11 Where in the USA was George almost photographed with Senator Gary Hart?
12 You cannot find the track 'Colour By Numbers' on the album of that name, but where can you find it?
13 What is the name of George's old school?
14 What is the name of the club where Culture Club did their first gig?
15 Where was the club where Culture Club did their first gig?
16 Who was Culture Club's first lead guitarist?
17 What is the name of the designer who developed the first Culture Club 'look' with George?
18 What was the name of the shop run by the designer who developed the Culture Club 'look' with George?
19 Where does Dexter Wong come from?
20 What is the name of Culture Club's producer?
21 George has four brothers and one sister. Can you name them?
22 Name at least five of the twelve cities in which Culture Club played in the USA in the spring of 1984?
23 What is the sport that both Jon and George learnt as children?
24 In what sport did Mikey excel at school?
25 Which member of Culture Club is married?
26 What is the maiden name of the wife of the married member of Culture Club?
27 Upon what date did the wedding of the married member of Culture Club take place?
28 What is the name of the mutual acquaintance who first put George in touch with Jon?
29 Who is the bass player in Culture Club?
30 Can you name the street in London where the famous 'Squat' was located?
31 What are the names of three of the London clubs George frequented in the pre-Culture Club days?
32 Which country did George visit the first time he travelled outside England?
33 Which member of the band is interested in photography?
34 Which two members of the band are clients of Antenna, the hairdressers in Kensington?
35 What company specially made footwear for Boy George?
36 Where did George get the famous black hat from?
37 What recording company approached George to become a solo artist in the days before Culture Club got together?
38 What name did George go under when he was with BowWowWow?
39 Can you name three of the groups Jon played with before he joined Culture Club?
40 How many weeks did 'Do You Really Want To Hurt Me?' remain at Number One in the UK charts?
41 How did Boy George surprise people when he returned to England after a holiday at the end of July 1984?
42 Who said he would like to adopt Boy George?
43 Which country made a big fuss about letting Boy George in?
44 With which record company are Culture Club signed?
45 What award did George win in 1983 and again in 1984?
46 What is Tony Gordon's job with Culture Club?
47 For whom has Boy George written songs, apart from Culture Club?
48 What is George's father's work?
49 What is the name of Helen Terry's debut single?
50 Who is George's favourite member of the Royal Family?

THE ANSWERS

1. George Alan O'Dowd.
2. Do You Really Want To Hurt Me?
3. Roy Hay.
4. Roy Hay.
5. Jon Moss.
6. 11th September 1957.
7. Eltham, South London.
8. Jon and George.
9. 'Karma Chameleon'.
10. It sold a million.
11. Pittsburgh.
12. On the B side of the 'Victims' single.
13. Eltham Green Comprehensive.
14. Crocs.
15. Rayleigh, Essex.
16. John Suede.
17. Susan Clowes.
18. The Foundry.
19. Malaysia.
20. Steve Levine.
21. Richard, Keith, Gerald, David, Siobhan.
22. Buffalo, Pittsburgh, Detroit, Cleveland, Milwaukee, St Paul, St Louis, Nashville, Atlanta, Charlotte, Lakeland, Miami Beach.
23. Boxing.
24. Football.
25. Roy Hay.
26. Alison Green.
27. 24th December 1982.
28. Kirk Brandon

29. Mikey Craig.
30. Carburton Street.
31. Heaven, Hell, Billy's, Blitz, Planets, Beat Route, Foobert's, Bangs, Visuals, Roxy, Shaguarama's, Louise's, Global Village.
32. Egypt.
33. Jon Moss.
34. George and Roy.
35. Puma.
36. It was a Christmas present from a friend.
37. EMI.
38. Lieutenant Lush.
39. Phone Bone Boulevard aka Pastrami Barmy aka Eskimo Norbert, The Clash, London, The Damned, The Edge aka Jane Ayre and The Belvederes.
40. Fifteen.
41. He returned with blond hair.
42. Robert Mitchum.
43. France.
44. Virgin Records.
45. Daily Mirror Reader's Award: Outstanding Music Personality.
46. Manager.
47. Petula Clark, Joe Cocker, Musical Youth, Helen Terry.
48. Builder.
49. 'Love Lies Lost'.
50. The Princess of Wales.

CULTURE CLUBOGRAPHY

7" SINGLES	RELEASE DATE	NOTES
White Boy/Love Twist	21.05.82	Also 12" single.
I'm Afraid Of Me/Murder Rap Trap	25.06.82	Also 12" single.
Do You Really Want To Hurt Me?/dub version	03.09.82	Also 12" single which includes 'Love Is Cold (You Were Never So Good)' and 7" picture disc. No. 1 on 19.10.82 and was No. 1 for 15 weeks.
Time (Clock Of The Heart/White Boys Can't Control It	19.11.82	Also 12" single which includes 'Romance Beyond The Alphabet' and 7" picture disc. No. 3 on 14.12.82 and was No. 3 for 5 weeks.
Church Of The Poison Mind/Man Shake	01.04.83	Also 12" single which includes 'Mystery Boy' and 7" picture disc. No. 2 on 11.4.83.
Karma Chameleon/That's The Way	05.09.83	Also 12" single 'Karma Chameleon' (7" mix) with 'I'll Tumble 4 Ya' (US 12" mix) and 7" picture disc. No. 1 on 20.9.83 and was No. 1 for 8 weeks.
Victims/Colour By Numbers	28.11.83	Also 12" single which includes 'Romance Revisited' and 7" picture disc. No. 3 on 20.12.83.
It's A Miracle/Love Twist (Live)	12.03.84	Also 12" single which contains 'It's A Miracle' and 'Miss Me Blind' (multi-mix), 'Love Twist' (live) and 'Melting Pot' (live) and 7" picture disc. No. 4 on 27.3.84 and No. 1 in April 1984.
War Song/Spanish version	24.09.84	Also 12" version which contains extended version and 7" version and Spanish version.

ALBUMS

Kissing To Be Clever	08.10.82	
Colour By Numbers	15.10.83	Compact disc 28.11.83, picture disc 6.12.83.

COMING (at the time of writing):

Waking Up With The House On Fire	End of October 1984.

FILM MUSIC

Two tracks for ELECTRIC DREAMS (Virgin Films/20th Century Fox, August 1984): 'Love Is Love' and 'The Dream'.

VIDEOS

Do You Really Want To Hurt Me?
Time (Clock Of The Heart).
I'll Tumble 4 Ya.
Church Of The Poison Mind.
Victims.
It's A Miracle.
Miss Me Blind (available USA only at time of writing).
A Kiss Across The Ocean (video mixed by Jon Moss of a Christmas concert live at the Odeon, Hammersmith, London, 1983).

FAN CLUB

Multicultural Club, PO Box 40, Ruislip, HA4 7ND, England.

DEDICATION AND ACKNOWLEDGMENTS

This book is dedicated to Culture Club fans everywhere, in the hope that it will please them.

Many people gave me a lot of their time and help in compiling this story of England's latest major pop phenomenon. In particular I should like to thank Judith Craig, Eleanor Donaldson and Tina at Antenna, Nicola Gill (moral support), Jan Gill (no relation!), Sue Leighton (very much), Kate Neville, Fiona Page, Mick Pickup, Neil Spencer and Karen Walter of *New Musical Express*, Joe Steeples and Stephen White.

THE AUTHOR

Anton Gill was born in Ilford, Essex and educated at Chigwell and Clare College, Cambridge. He has worked as an actor, playwright and director, in England, West Germany and Switzerland, and he has written several plays and features for the BBC and for various European radio stations. He is also the author of two novels, and one other work of non-fiction, *Martin Allen is Missing*. Anton Gill lives in south London with his wife, Nicola, and a small ill-tempered cat.

ILLUSTRATION CREDITS

Alpha 6, 66, 80, 84; Associated Press Ltd 22; Calandra Balfour 112; Michael Balfour 22; BBC Publications Ltd 78; Eric Bouvet 82; George Caspari Inc, New York 21, 41, 63, 73, 101, 111; Alan Davidson 9, 19, 91, 104; Hermione Eyre 110; Daniel Farson 96; Anton Gill 53; James Hamilton 22; Robert Harding 89; Paul Jacquet, Brussels 13, 79; Kartos Montecatini Terme 91; Independent Television Publications Ltd 102; London Features International Ltd 21, 34, 36; Laura McNair-Wilson 116; The Medici Society 119; Omnibus Press Ltd 36; Pictor International – London 71; Pictorial Press Ltd 6, 31, 51, 55, 58, 64, 65, 79; Punch Publications Ltd 103; Record Winner! Publishing Ltd 102; Rex Features Ltd 6, 43, 50, 63, 111; Derek Ridgers 32, 33, 56, 57; Stan M Rosenlund 97; Rossler Papier 31, 51; Johnny Rosza 2; Pia Tryde Sandeman 86; Terry Seago 6; Frank Spooner Pictures 6, 73, 74, 113; Syndication International Ltd 13, 16, 45, 47, 49, 69, 77, 108, 114, 119, 121; Richard Young 41, 101; Daily Mail 29
Front Cover David Parker

NOTE
The information in this book is, as far as it was possible to ascertain, correct at the time of writing. Apologies to all if this proves not to be the case. A.G.